SANCTIFICATION AND COUNSELING

- *Growing by Grace: Sanctification and Counseling*
- *Is All Truth God's Truth?*
- *Joyfully Counseling People with New Hearts*

Jay E. Adams

Institute for Nouthetic Studies, a ministry of Mid-America Baptist Theological Seminary, 2095 Appling Road, Cordova, TN 38016
mabts.edu / nouthetic.org / INSBookstore.com

Sanctification and Counseling by Jay E. Adams
Copyright © 2020 by the Institute for Nouthetic Studies

ISBN: 9781949737110 (print)
9781949737127 (eBook)

Editor: Donn R. Arms
Design: James Wendorf | www.FaithfulLifePublishers.com

Previously published as:
  Growing by Grace © 2003 by Jay E Adams
  Is All Truth God's Truth? © 2003 by Jay E Adams
  Joyfully Counseling People with New Hearts © by Jay E Adams

---

Library of Congress Cataloging-in-Publication Data
Names: Adams, Jay E., 1929-
Title: Sanctification and Counseling / Jay E. Adams
Description: Cordova: Institute for Nouthetic Studies, 2020
Identifiers: ISBN 9781949737110
Classification: LCC BV4012.2 | DDC 253.5

Unless otherwise noted, New Testament Bible quotations are taken from the Christian Counselor's New Testament and Proverbs, Institute for Nouthetic Studies, Cordova, TN © 2019.
© 1977, 1980, 1994. by Jay E. Adams.

All Old Testament quotations are taken from the NEW AMERICAN STANDARD BIBLE, © 1960, 1962, 1963, 1968, 1971, 1972, 1973, 1975, 1977, 1995 by The Lockman Foundation. Used by permission.

All rights reserved. No part of this publication may be reproduced, stored in a retrieval system, or transmitted in any form or by any means – electronic, mechanical, photocopy, recording, or any other – except for brief quotations in printed reviews, without prior permission of the publisher.

Published in the United States of America

Foreword

Jay Adams understood early on that if biblical counselors were to be effective in the counseling room, they must have a solid grasp of the key theological issue in counseling—the doctrine of Sanctification, the doctrine that explains how believers grow and change.

Because this doctrine is of vital importance, and because counselors who do not have this doctrine straight would surely fail in their efforts to help people in a way that pleases God, Adams devoted a large section to it in his foundational theology book.[1] Several years later, realizing that a section in one book was insufficient to press home the importance of a clear understanding of Sanctification, he wrote an entire book demonstrating how it is Scripture, skillfully used by the counselor, that brings about God-pleasing change.[2]

During the years that followed, as Adams traveled and interacted with counselors, and read books being promoted to biblical counselors, he grew increasingly concerned that this vital doctrine was not being taught well to the next generation of counseling students. Counselors were being urged to probe their counselees for "heart idols," some were teaching a form of antinomianism under the banner of "gospel sanctification" and others continued to insist that secular psychological concepts were important compliments to a "Bible only" counseling approach.

---

1 *More than Redemption, A Theology of Christian Counseling*, 1979.
2 *How to Help People Change*, 1986.

Then in 2002, a journal that Adams had founded and served as editor for over 15 years, published two articles directly challenging several core aspects of the doctrine of Sanctification as Adams had laid out in his books, and had been teaching for decades. For Adams, it was time to do what he could to address this drift. He took up his pen and produced the three books you have in your hands—combined into one volume.

In the first, *Growing by Grace: Sanctification and Counseling*, Adams explains the doctrine with his trademark clarity and focus and shows why a clear understanding is vital to effective counseling. A careful study of this short book will relieve any earnest biblical counselor of confusion on the subject.

The second book, *Is All Truth God's Truth?*, confronts a common assault on the means of our Sanctification, the Scriptures. Under the slogan "All truth is God's truth," the doctrine of the sufficiency of the Scriptures has been challenged by those who would insist on incorporating the "discoveries" of secular psychological theorists in the counseling room.

The third book, *Joyfully Counseling People with New Hearts*, answers the charge that Nouthetic counselors deal only with outward behavior and ignore issues of the heart. Adams vehemently denies this and demonstrates that it is the biblical/nouthetic counselor alone who truly deals with the heart.

All three books were published independently as *Ministry Monographs for Modern Times*. It is our prayer that by bringing them together into one volume, they will enjoy a wider readership and that biblical counselors would embrace a truly biblical understanding of the doctrine of Sanctification and how it is worked out in the counseling room.

Donn R Arms, *Director*
Institute for Nouthetic Studies

Sanctification and Counseling

Table of Contents

Growing by Grace: Sanctification and Counseling..........................7
Is All Truth God's Truth?..107
Joyfully Counseling People with New Hearts..............................171

Growing by Grace

Sanctification and Counseling

Jay E. Adams

"But grow by the grace and the knowledge of our Lord and Savior Jesus Christ."

II Peter 3:18

Contents

Introduction 11
Why There is a Need for Sanctification 13
What is Sanctification Anyway? 19
What Makes Sanctification Possible? 28
How is Sanctification Effected? 36
The Spirit, Sanctification, and Counseling 42
The Human Factor in Sanctification 47
Sanctification and the Word 51
Let's Talk about Counseling 57
Common Territory 62
Nouthetic Counseling Is Unique 69
Discipleship 74
Grow by Grace 80
How Much Growth Is Possible? 86
Does Suffering Sanctify? 90
Sanctification and Obedience 97
Conclusion 105

Introduction

At the outset, I want to explain why I have placed sanctification and counseling in juxtaposition in this book. To some (particularly those who believe in eclectic counseling) it may seem odd – indeed, even foolish – to do so. To those who believe in biblical counseling, however, the explanation that I shall give will doubtless make sense.

I chose to consider the relationship of sanctification to counseling in order to determine the implications for counseling that may arise. It is biblical counseling, then, that is the concern of the book; the scriptural teaching about sanctification is of concern only as it throws light upon the practice of nouthetic[1] counseling.

My emphasis upon counseling, however, must in no way be understood as downplaying the care that has been taken in discussing the biblical truths concerning sanctification. Without

---

1 For those not familiar with the term, the word "nouthetic" is a transliteration of a word in the Greek New Testament, which is found particularly in the writings of the Apostle Paul. The Greek word, nouthesia, was brought over into English because it is larger than the English term "counsel" and because it is free from many of the unwanted associations that the word "counsel" carries. Nouthesia contains three elements; it speaks of change that is brought about by verbal confrontation out of concern for the one who is counseled. In this book, for the sake of convenience, unless otherwise indicated, the word "counsel" is used interchangeably with the word nouthesia. For more detail, consult my book *Competent to Counsel*.

adequate attention given to the exposition of this pivotal doctrine, its implications for counseling would be flawed. It is, therefore, possible to study the doctrine of sanctification itself as I have set it forth here as well as to study how this teaching impinges upon biblical counseling. All doctrine has important implications for counseling, but I think you will see why I have called sanctification pivotal to pastoral counseling.

"Okay, what you have done is clear. But why do it? What is the great significance that sanctification has for counseling?"

This question is legitimate. Of course, since this book is concerned precisely with setting forth the implications of the doctrine for counseling, in one sense, the entire book is my answer to that question. Allow me to summarize in the introduction why I have written this book.

Because counseling is so intimately connected to sanctification, if one's understanding of sanctification is faulty, that will negatively affect his counseling. Because counseling is an aspect of sanctification, or because in so many situations it is so important to proper Christian growth, sanctification often depends upon effective, biblical counseling. In short, the two are so closely bound together that counseling cannot be properly carried on apart from a correct understanding of sanctification. And in those cases where biblical counseling is required, sanctification will not take place as it should unless the correct relationship and implications of each are understood and properly worked out. In other words, each depends upon the other. Given that fact, I think you will agree that it is altogether appropriate to study the symbiotic relationship between counseling and sanctification.

Chapter One

Why There is a Need for Sanctification

Through one representative act of rebellion, Adam plunged the entire human race into sin. By eating the forbidden fruit, he caused two things to happen: from birth all men (Jesus excepted) became guilty and all men became corrupt. God deals with *guilt* by the *act* of *justifying* those who believe the gospel, and He deals with *corruption* by the *process* of *sanctifying* them. Sanctification is needed, therefore, because of man's corruption.

What does it mean that all are born corrupt (or polluted)? Essentially, it means that human nature has been so warped by sin that, apart from the grace of God freely granted to those God determines to save, men cannot do anything that pleases God.[2] As Paul put it in Romans 8:8: "Those who are in the flesh can't please God." Why is that?

The reason for this inability[3] is that the whole person, inner and outer, has become oriented away from God and His will, and his nature is now oriented toward sin. As Isaiah put it, both man's "ways" (outer words and actions) and "thoughts" (inner understanding, desires, and intents) are, in this manner, so distorted as to need radical

---
2 In Adam the intellectual and moral aspects of the "image of God" with which man was endowed by creation (Genesis 1:27) were lost and must be "renewed" (cf. Colossians 3:10; Ephesians 4:24).
3 In Greek, *ou dunetai*. *Ou* is a strong negative.

change: "For My thoughts are not your thoughts, neither are your ways My ways" (Isaiah 55:8). That is why God says, "Let the wicked forsake his way, and the unrighteous man his thoughts; and let him return to the LORD, and He will have compassion on him, and to our God, for He will abundantly pardon" (Isaiah 55:7). Clearly, God is displeased with both our ways and our thoughts – so much so that He calls for *repentance*: "forsake" and "return" are the two operative verbs in Isaiah 55, verse 7 quoted above.

The concept of repentance in the Old and the New Testaments includes both the inner and the outer elements. The Hebrew term *shuv* means both to "return" and "turn," referring to outer change that repentance effects; the Greek word *metanoieo* means "to rethink so as to change one's mind," and refers to inner change that brings about the turning. In other words, the former emphasizes the need for a change of ways, while the latter focuses upon the change in thinking that leads to the change of ways.

There are those who claim to have truly repented because either their *thinking* or their *behavior* (but not both) more or less conforms to God's Word, yet in God's sight, neither conforms. To understand or think differently, without a subsequent change in one's ways (behavior or way of life) means that the understanding and the thinking are superficial and ingenuine. On the other hand, to "change one's ways," without a change of heart which affects one's thoughts and intents, is pharisaical and equally unacceptable. In Isaiah 55, God makes it clear that the problem is twofold; it is an internal-outward problem. Thus, there must be a decided change in *both* areas of one's life. Since the whole person sins, the whole person must be changed. In another chapter, we shall see how that two-fold change takes place. But for now, let us consider further this need for sanctification as it pertains to fallen men and women.

Corruption of man's nature, as we have seen, makes him unable to please God in both his *thoughts* and his *ways*. Those two highly descriptive words are Isaiah's shorthand for all of human life. To speak of a person's thoughts and ways as unacceptable in God's eyes is to speak of him as *totally* unable to please Him.[4] Paul agrees with Isaiah. There is not one scintilla of holiness (or a desire for it) in human nature as it comes forth at birth. Nothing about it is oriented toward God or pleases Him. Rather, human beings are born corrupt persons who, because of this corruption, develop thoughts and ways that result in living "in the flesh." In Romans 8:4 and 5, Paul mentions walking according to the flesh and setting the mind on fleshly things. These words correspond to Isaiah's "ways" and "thoughts."

By "flesh" Paul refers to the lifestyle that is produced by the sinful nature. *If* an unbeliever were to desire or attempt to love and serve God (which he *would* not do), he *could* not do it. Why? Because his nature and his lifestyle (which, as we have seen, includes one's thoughts and ways) prohibit him from doing so. As a result, for a human being to please God he must have both a change of nature and a change of lifestyle.

The Holy Spirit alone can rectify this disastrous two-fold problem. He alone can change man's nature, and it is the Spirit, dwelling within the believer, Who fights successfully against the flesh throughout his life, thus enabling him to become more and more like Jesus Christ. The simple fact is that because the unbeliever does not possess the Spirit of Christ, he does not belong to Christ and

---

4   Total depravity means that every aspect of a person has been corrupted by the fall; it does not mean that he is as sinful as he might possibly become. It does mean, however, that there is nothing in a person's unregenerate nature which can or will respond favorably to the things of God (see I Corinthians 2:14). This fact is of extreme importance to biblical counselors, who should not knowingly counsel unbelievers. If unbelieving counselees do not please God by their present lifestyles (Romans 8:8), there is no biblical reason to help them develop different lifestyles that would be every bit as displeasing to Him. Indeed, it would be sin for the counselor to do so. Truly biblical counselors seek to evangelize unbelievers, not to counsel them.

cannot be considered one of God's sons. "If anybody doesn't have Christ's Spirit, he isn't His" (Romans 8:9; see also v. 14). These grave deficiencies (apart from a work of the Spirit in him subsequent to birth) make it impossible for him even to repent and believe the gospel. The work of the Spirit that enables him to do so is called the "new birth." When a person is born again,[5] the process of sanctification begins to take place. It is then and then alone that counseling may profitably be carried on.[6] So it is evident that sanctification occurs only in those who have had a change of nature and repented.

All of this is important for the counselor to know. Sanctification, as we shall see, involves both inner and outer growth toward holiness that is produced by the grace of God through His Holy Spirit.[7] Since the problem involves thoughts and ways that displease God, the remedy, as in repentance, must also reach to both aspects of the one who is being sanctified. The fruit of the Spirit, which of course means the products of His work in the believer, reveal qualities that are both inner and outer: "… the Spirit's fruit is love, joy, peace, patience, kindness, goodness, faithfulness, meekness, self-control" (Galatians 5:22, 23). Clearly, those qualities involve both inner and outer transformations in the person who, born only the first time, possesses none of them.[8]

---

[5] Or, as the word *anothen* possibly means, born "from above" (John 3:3, 7). But see John 3:4 where Nicodemus' words "a second time" seem to parallel *anothen*, indicating that "again" is the preferred translation of this word that, apart from context, may be translated either way.

[6] We shall consider what necessitates counseling at a later point in the book.

[7] In Romans 1:4, the Holy Spirit is called "the Spirit of holiness" because it is His work to produce holiness. Sanctification comes only through Him.

[8] The world speaks of these things as though men may possessthem apart from the work of the Spirit, but what the world describes by the misuse of these labels are qualities that are actually quite different from the fruit of the Spirit. His fruit is (continued on the next page)

Note also that it is not merely the change of one's orientation that brings about the new sanctified lifestyle. Changed thinking and living depend not only upon the working of the Spirit as He applies His Word,[9] but also upon Him as He cooperates with the believer, motivating and enabling him to work out the possibilities of the new nature and the new lifestyle that is developing.[10] You can see, then, that the process which we call sanctification is not simple but complex. The counselor must not only understand the process, but also must know how to work with counselees in such a manner that he does not overlook any aspect of it, or overemphasize one to the detriment of the rest. There is always the temptation to do so. Knowledge of the ins and outs of sanctification will go a long way toward helping him to resist the temptation.

Change is not brought about by the counselor or by the counselee alone; change is a divine/human activity. All of these factors, as you can see, make it vital for the biblical counselor to understand and, as he counsels, to continually remember all the elements of the process.

So then, while the need for sanctification is great, the need to understand and appreciate it fully is equally important. Without this process at work in the life of the believer, his lifestyle following

---

always positively related to God on a vertical level; the former (in contrast) are humanistically related to man on a purely horizontal one. This distinction points to the quite different characters that Christians develop from those that are found in non-Christians. Moreover, their worldviews – which affect all they do and think – are quite distinct. And because the love, joy, peace, and so on, that pagan counseling systems claim to bring about are ersatz, the biblical counselor will not be duped into believing that the methods proposed in these systems will produce that which, according the Scriptures is due solely to sanctification by the Spirit.

9   See also John 17:17, "Sanctify them by the truth; Your Word is truth!"
10 See also Philippians 2:13: "…it is God Who is producing in you both the willingness and the ability to do the things that please Him."

the new birth would not be unlike that which he lived before it. So since we agree on that – don't we? – let's proceed with our study.

Chapter Two

What is Sanctification Anyway?

We have seen already that sanctification is needed to deal with the scourge of corruption inherited from our first father, Adam.[11] We have learned that sanctification is not the same as justification: justification is an instantaneous act that deals with the guilt of our sin, while sanctification is an ongoing process that deals with the corruption that leads us into more and more sin. Like repentance, which has to do with both inner and outer factors, so too sanctification is a two-fold process that relates to both the inner and the outer lifestyle – how one thinks and how he acts. So far, so good. But what, precisely, is sanctification?

Let's begin by taking a look at the biblical terms associated with sanctification, which themselves tell us a lot about the process. The Greek words *hagiasmos* (sanctification, holiness), *hagiazo* (to sanctify) and *hagios* (holy) are terms that all refer to that which is "separated." The separation envisioned is both *from* sin and Satan and *to* God and righteousness.

In writing to the church, the Apostle Peter said, "…[you] are chosen according to the foreknowledge of God the Father, that *by*

---

11 In addition to which, as a result of that corruption, we have contributed to the human legacy of sin by means of our own attitudes and acts. But each develops his own individual style of sinning. So, not only must the corruption of our nature, but also the lifestyles that each has developed as the outworking of that corruption, be overcome.

the Spirit's sanctification[12] you may obey…" (I Peter 1:2; emphasis mine). Paul wrote, "Now this is God's will: your sanctification" (I Thessalonians 4:3), and "God didn't call us to uncleanness, but rather to sanctification" (I Thessalonians 4:7). Thus in Romans 6:19b he explained,

> In the same way that you presented your members as slaves to uncleanness and lawlessness to bring about more lawlessness, now you must present your members as slaves of righteousness to bring about sanctification.

And, as a final sample of New Testament usage, consider Paul's benediction:

> May the God of peace Himself sanctify you completely; may your entire being – spirit and soul and body – be kept blameless for the coming of our Lord Jesus Christ (I Thessalonians 5:23).

Obviously, as you can see from these few New Testament citations, sanctification is an important matter that extends to the whole of life. The Christian is, as Paul said, "called to sanctification." Becoming sanctified is a lifelong task assigned to every believer by virtue of becoming a believer. Sanctification, then, is an integral part of the Christian life.

The Old Testament term *qadosh* (sanctified, holy) and those derivatives from it, bear essentially the same meaning as the New Testament words, though because of temple ritual and Mosaic law there is a vast application of sanctification to things, places, events, times, and so forth, that is not found in the New Testament. The word refers to persons whose lives are consecrated (separated) to God, or of things (such as the pots and pans used in the temple) set apart for sacred uses. In Numbers 7:1, we read that Moses "… finished setting up the tabernacle and had anointed and sanctified

---

12 See also Romans 15:16: "in order that the offering up of the Gentiles may be acceptable, being sanctified by the Holy Spirit."

it with all its equipment, including the altar and its utensils which he likewise anointed and sanctified..."¹³ (Berkeley). In all such instances, the sanctification, or setting aside, is a one-time thing (though the effects were lasting), whereas the personal sanctification with which we are principally concerned in this book is a growth process.

Prophetically speaking of Jesus' resurrection, David wrote, "You will not leave My soul in sheol, nor will you allow Your Holy One to see corruption" (Psalm 16:10, NKJV). God, and His Son, of course, were always set apart as the only true God and therefore quite distinct (holy, i.e., separate) from all other (false) gods. There is nothing progressive about Their set-apart-ness.

That which was "holy" in the Mosaic law was distinguished from that which was "common" or "unclean" (cf. Leviticus 10:10). Although sanctification in the Old Testament most often referred to ritual or ceremonial holiness rather than holiness of lifestyle, the intent of this set-apart, godly relationship of things and people was to symbolize the spiritual relationship that is more clearly spelled out in the New Testament. The clean/unclean system of the Old Testament was intended to teach that all of life (what you eat, what you wear, etc.) is to be consecrated (set apart) to God. That teaching is one that counselors today must continue to inculcate in counselees.

As the Old Testament priest was holy (Leviticus 21:6), so now that all believers are declared to be priests, they too are considered holy (I Peter 2:5, N.B. the designation a *"holy* priesthood"). In fact, every Christian, by virtue of his justification before God, is considered a "saint" (cf. Philippians 1:1), or "holy one." That is to say, by a once-for-all act of God, he has been *set apart* from others to love and serve God. Thus, the New Testament does not entirely abandon the idea of groups or individuals being set apart

---

13   These items, thus, were *set aside* for special use, and that use alone.

once-for-all by one definitive act of sanctification.[14] It is important, then, to distinguish those verses that speak of sanctification in the definitive Old Testament sense from those that speak of progressive sanctification in the New Testament sense. Often the progressive sense of sanctification is spoken of in terms of "growing," "learning," and the like (II Peter 3:18; Titus 3:14) rather than by the use of words such as "sanctified."

This definitive, instantaneous Old Testament "setting apart" in name and status is but a precursor of what God expects the believer to *become*.[15] Unlike the Old Testament pot or pan that was set apart for temple use, the New Testament "saint," designated as such at conversion, must become saintly[16] (something that the lifeless, inert thing could not do). In other words, the "saint" is one who has been "set apart" (positionally) for the purpose of becoming "set apart" (in his actual lifestyle). He is to live up to his status more and more.

Sanctification, then, is a significant matter. No counselor can safely fail to understand that his counseling is intended to assist counselees in this process of becoming more thoroughly set apart (sanctified). Anything that does not contribute to growth from

---

14 See also Hebrews 10:14: "By a single offering He has perfected for all time those who are being set apart." In this verse the once-for-all "perfecting" (the granting of a perfect or completed status before God) that occurs at the time of justification is contrasted with the on-going process of "being set apart" (as one grows by grace in this life). In the verse, the verb used is *teleioo* (note the contrast with verse 1 where it also occurs).
15 The word "marriage" may refer to the legal ceremony in which one becomes "man and wife," or to all that follows. Similarly, the word "sanctification" may refer to the legal relationship (status) established by God at justification or to all that follows.
16 That is, more and more set apart from sin and to righteousness in his thinking and ways (see the discussion of Isaiah 55:8 in chapter 1).

sinful thought and behavior to righteous thinking and ways of living has no part in counseling.

It is wise for counselors to learn about the definitive and the progressive aspects of sanctification so as to be able to call upon counselees to approximate in daily living what they are reckoned to be before God. In Romans 6:11, Paul wrote, "So too you must count [or reckon] yourselves to be dead to sin, but living for God in Christ Jesus." Again, in this verse, the two aspects of salvation – that which is reckoned (counted; one's status before God) and that which we are in the process of becoming – appear in relation to one another. "You are dead," Paul is saying, "so live in that light. Sin has been put aside once-for-all in Christ (though not in your daily 'living'). That means that daily you are obligated to live up to your status. So I am exhorting you to live more and more for God instead of for sin."

"How should one live?" a counselee may ask. The astute counselor answers, "According to your status as a saint," or words to that effect. Indeed, because of the *what-you-are/what-you-must-become* dynamic found everywhere in the New Testament, you may go on to tell your counselee, "You see, by telling you how He regards you – what you have become in Christ – and because God has spelled this out not only by the teachings of the Bible but also by the example of His Son, He has made it clear that by His grace you are capable of growing into the 'stature' of Jesus Christ" (Ephesians 4:13).

Look at the sixth chapter of Romans a bit more carefully. Here, Paul's concern is to show the inconsistency of "continuing in sin." It is inconsistent for the Christian to do so, he argues, because grace has transformed both the believer's status (standing) before God and his ability to live righteously. All of this he has been explaining in the previous chapter. In chapter 5:20, Paul points out that grace is more than a match for sin: "Where sin abounded, grace far more abounded." So, he asks in chapter 6:1, "Should we continue in sin so that grace might abound?" The thought runs this way: someone might think, "if grace covers all sin, then why not sin all the more so that there will be an even greater abundance of grace to cover it?" But that is absurd, he responds (v. 2). After all, in God's reckoning, "you have died to sin" – that is your status before Him. How then can you even *think* of living in sin? Then comes his clinching argument.

The argument that backs up his statement in verse 2 is this: Don't you know that you were baptized into Christ and what the implications of that fact are?[17] Presumably, some would say, "I guess I don't." Well, let me tell you about it, is Paul's retort. By being baptized into Christ, you were baptized into His death. Note that the verse doesn't speak of being baptized into water, but of being baptized into *Christ*. That distinction is important.

But what does it mean to be baptized into Christ? Paul goes on to explain. By being baptized into Christ, you were baptized into Christ's *death*, which is what I have been talking about – because you *died* by virtue of being "in Christ," you are considered to have *died* to sin. By this baptism into Christ, Paul goes on to explain, you were baptized into His death, His burial, and His resurrection (v. 4). And just as being baptized into Christ means that you were baptized into His death, so too being baptized into Him means being baptized into His resurrection. And that means that God reckons you to have been raised to a new lifestyle ("newness of life"). So your baptism into Christ implies death to the old lifestyle and life to the new one.

Now, the importance of the phrase "baptized into Christ" is that God "counts" (or "reckons") you to have experienced all of these things that *He* experienced. Paul's favorite phrase, "in Christ," used throughout his letters, corresponds to the concept he sets

---

17 Many counselees don't know this because they were never taught it. So it is wise for a counselor to learn Paul's argument and, from time to time, to use it to encourage righteous living.

forth here: those who are "in Christ" are considered such by virtue of being "baptized" *into* Him. The word "baptize" (*baptizo*) has been wrongly interpreted to mean "to dip" (that is, to put into and *remove*); there is another word (bapto) that carries the meaning "to dip."[18] The word *baptizo* ("baptize"), on the other hand, means "to put together, to unite." The idea behind *baptizo* in this text then, is to place things together *so as to stay together*. That understanding is plainly in view in this passage in Romans where the believer is thought of as *united* and *identified with* Christ. There is no idea of dipping him into Christ and removing him once again.[19] Precisely the opposite! The idea of such a union with Christ is that he remains in Him: all that He has done is attributed to the believer as if he had experienced it himself.

So Paul says, in effect, "If you have the whole (baptism into Christ) – *all* that Christ experienced – you have the part of that whole that corresponds to what I am teaching." By virtue of being baptized into Christ, the Christian is reckoned to have been circumcised with Christ (Colossians 2:11, 12), crucified with Christ (Galatians 2:20), to have died, been buried, and been raised with Christ (Romans 6:4) and to be seated with Him in heavenly places at the right hand of the Father (Colossians 3:1; Ephesians 2:6). The whole of Christ's work is attributed to the believer because he is identified with (baptized into) Him.

---

18 Bapto, "to dip," is found in Luke 16:24.
19 See also I Corinthians 12:13 where the believer is said to have been baptized (baptizo) by the Spirit into the body of Christ (the invisible church). Certainly, one isn't dipped into the body of Christ and then removed! Rather, by the Spirit he is "united" or "joined" with God's church. This concept of being "united, joined, and identified with" is the essence of baptism (cf. I Corinthians 10:2, where the Israelites were baptized "into Moses"). Baptism with water is the uniting ordinance; one joins the visible church by water baptism as he joins the invisible church by Spirit baptism.

Growing by Grace: Sanctification and Counseling

Because this vital biblical concept is foreign even to many counselors, let me take the time to make it as clear as I can by means of an illustration. If I place a bean "into" a jar, the bean is "in" the jar and, as a result, identified with it. Wherever the jar goes, the bean also goes because it was introduced *into* the jar and now is *in* the jar. Put the jar on a table, the bean is on the table. Place the jar on the floor, the bean is on the floor. Raise it up to a shelf and the bean is raised up as well – all because the bean is *in the jar*. Just so, the Christian is viewed as going through all that Christ did by virtue of being united with Him (cf. Romans 6:5)[20] by Spirit[21] baptism.

Paul emphasizes death, burial, and resurrection not because baptism into Christ means only that, but rather, because it pictures entrance into the whole of Christ's experiences, including baptism into His death and resurrection, which is the point that he is making in the passage. He is saying that, if you are counted to have died, been buried, and risen with Christ to newness of life, then live like it! Live the new life that you have in Him; let your everyday life more closely approximate your status before God.

So in this passage, and in many more like it, you see that the essence of sanctification is simply this: becoming what you are. That is to say, becoming in daily life what you are already reckoned to be by virtue of being in Christ.[22] This process is a daily

---

20 "If we have become united with Him in a death like His…" (emphasis mine). Here Paul explains in unmistakable terms that being baptized into Christ is being "united with Him."
21 Plainly, there is not a drop of water in Romans 6. To introduce the idea of water baptism into the passage is to intrude it rather than find it there. Water baptism certainly does not produce the results of which Paul speaks, but Spirit baptism does.
22 The whole put on/put off dynamic found in Ephesians 4 and Colossians 3 (and detailed in my book The Christian Counselor's Manual) is a further example of this approach to sanctification. Paul says in effect that in Christ you are a (continued on the next page)

one, as we shall see later on; but it is the dynamic by which every nouthetic counselor encourages the believer to grow out of his sinful thoughts and ways into God's righteous thoughts and ways. Sanctification thus provides the pattern for discipleship, change during counseling, and daily growth.

---

new person; so now, in everyday life, put off the old person that you were, along with his sinful ways, and put on the new person that you have become in Christ with His new, holy ways.

Chapter Three
What Makes Sanctification Possible?

Obviously, since people are by birth unable to please God,[23] and therefore are not proper subjects for counseling, something must intervene before an individual may be accepted for counseling. What is it? Plainly, he must become a Christian.

But to speak of one becoming a Christian is not like saying that he has become a member of a political party or even a partner in a business. Becoming a disciple of Jesus Christ is a decision that is made not wholly by the person himself. Given his inability and his adverse orientation, what enables him to turn in the opposite direction, repent, and believe the gospel? In asking that, we are probing the more ultimate question – "Why is it that one person becomes a Christian and another does not?"

Jesus answered that question when He spoke about the Father "drawing" people to Him (John 6:44). And He enlarged the point

---

23 See also Psalm 51:5; 58:3; Ephesians 2:3. This last reference, in which Paul says that "by nature we too were children of wrath," is interesting. In Greek usage, and elsewhere in the New Testament (I Corinthians 11:14), phusis (nature) does not always mean "determined by genetic code," but rather, "things as they are without anything being done to make them so." It is the person or thing as it (he) is in itself (himself). One does not have to do anything to make himself a child of wrath. Indeed, unless something is done to him, he simply (or by nature) is such.

What Makes Sanctification Possible?

in speaking about His death on the cross when He said that by being "lifted up" He would "draw all sorts of people"[24] to Himself (John 12:32). In other words, His sacrificial, penal, substitutionary death would be the occasion for the drawing. These verses unmistakably teach that in order to transform one's wholly corrupt nature there must be the imposition of an outside Force. That drawing power is the effectual force of the Holy Spirit.

In the Bible there are various way of picturing this transforming imposition. We have already noted Jesus' words to Nicodemus, "You must be born again." Consider this passage for a minute. John the Baptist came calling people to repentance. As a sign of repentance, he baptized with water those who repented. Jesus, however, came baptizing with the Spirit (In John 1:33, the Baptist himself sets forth the contrast). Nicodemus came as a representative of[25] the Pharisees (John 3:1). The Pharisees refused to repent and be baptized by John (Luke 7:30; John 3:11, 12). Thus, when Jesus spoke of being baptized with water and with the Spirit (John 3:5), He meant that they must repent[26] and believe in Him.

---

24 The verb, elko, means "to draw, drag, and pull," and clearly refers to the exertion of an outside force (not necessarily hostile or resisted). The phrase "all sorts of people," as I have translated it in the CCNT, is more accurate than the KJV which has "all men." Elsewhere, John put it this way in the book of Revelation when he spoke of the redeemed being "from every nation and tribe and people and tongue" (Revelation 7:9). For more on this important matter, see my book Christian Living in the World.

25 The word "of" probably ought to have the force of an ablative and be translated "from."

26 The "water" in John 3:5 stands for the meaning and purpose of John's baptism: repentance (Mark 1:4). Jesus did not mean that water baptism brought about any inner change; it was a sign that it had already taken place.

Jesus spoke to Nicodemus both as a representative and as an individual. Note the important interplay of singulars and plurals. In addition to speaking to Nicodemus as an individual, Jesus said, "you *all* [all of you Pharisees] must be born again" (v. 7). And He also spoke not only of Himself alone (using "I"), but also of John and Himself together (note the use of "we" and "our" as well in v. 11). The Pharisees had refused to believe in John or in Jesus, who jointly came proclaiming God's message. Evidence of unbelief in John's message was their refusal to be baptized by him. Rather than follow the example of his fellow Pharisees, who rejected what John and he said, Jesus urged Nicodemus to believe and receive both baptisms (John 3:5).

Now this new birth into a new kind of life is produced, as Jesus explained, by the Holy Spirit: "what is born of the Spirit is spirit" (John 3:6). That is to say, spiritual life is produced by His action in the inner person. The Spirit is the outer Force Who brings about the inner change. As Paul said, "God's love has been poured into our hearts through the Holy Spirit Who was given to us" (Romans 5:5). This statement and the words of Jesus to Nicodemus appear to be references to the prophecy of Ezekiel who wrote,

> I will sprinkle clean water upon you, and you will be cleansed from all your impurities.... A new heart, too, I will give you, and a new spirit I will put within you. I will take the heart of stone out of your flesh, and I will give you a heart of flesh. I will put My Spirit within you and cause you to walk in My statutes, and you shall observe My ordinances and do them (Ezekiel 36:25–27, Berkeley).

As the Agent of the Father, the Spirit does what a person cannot do for himself: He transforms unregenerate persons into regenerate ones. He changes the "heart" so that the whole person is now oriented toward God and toward doing His commandments (v. 27). The "new spirit," that which is "born of the Spirit" (John

3:6) is an attitude of acceptance and desire to do what God wills. The old heart was stony. That means that it was impervious and resistant to the things of God. It was cold, hard, and lifeless. Now the newly implanted heart that replaces the one that the Spirit removed is warm, alive to spiritual things, and open to the teachings of God's Word.

A slightly different way of expressing these ideas is found in Ephesians 2:1, 4, and 5, where Paul pictures the transformation in terms of the resurrection of those who were "dead in trespasses and sins." He speaks of those who were spiritually dead being "made alive" (v. 5). The outside Force that raises the spiritually dead, according to Ephesians 2:4, once more is identified as God, the Spirit, Who, in doing so, is motivated by love. Throughout the New Testament, the very close concepts of new life and resurrection from the death of sin to live for Christ are used to portray this change of disposition toward, and a new ability to do, God's will.

Akin to the images of being born again and being spiritually raised to newness of life is that of becoming a new creature (or creation) in Christ. Paul wrote, "Accordingly, if anybody is in Christ, he is a new creation; everything old has passed away; see, new things have come into being" (II Corinthians 5:17).[27] The problem of corruption could only be dealt with in a radical way, as these three expressions show. Apart from a new birth, resurrection, or a new creation – expressions bold enough to express the radical nature of regeneration – the individual would retain all of his old ways.

Paul is speaking of the new status, the new orientation, and the new abilities that the regenerated person has been given by the Spirit. Note as well, further along in the fifth chapter of II

---

27 The "new creation" that the Christian becomes in Christ foreshadows the new creation of Revelation 21 and 22. There, too, old things have passed away, and all things are new (see especially Revelation 21:1, 4, 5).

Corinthians, Paul adds, "For our sake He made Him Who didn't know sin to be sin, so that we might become God's righteousness by Him" (v. 21). God looked on His Son as a sin-offering, bearing our sin, so that He may look on us as possessing all His righteousness! That is the new status we have in justification. It is remarkable! Too much to express! But everywhere you turn in the New Testament, you discover that God has taken pains to show the radical change that regeneration makes. And everywhere the new, perfect righteousness – the new status – is held up as an incentive to live in accordance with it. A concise statement of this is found in Ephesians 4:1: "I urge you to walk in a way that is appropriate to the calling to which you were called."

So what do we call this transformation of our natures? Traditionally, theologians have called it "regeneration" (being made alive by a new birth), thus carrying on the concept of birth that leads to a new life. Some of us prefer to call it "quickening" (or the granting of spiritual life to a spiritually dead person). But whatever biblical figure of speech one uses, God is speaking of a change leading to the desire and the ability to please Him – something that is made possible by His transforming power (cf. Philippians 2:13). It is only because of this wholly gracious act of transformation that the regenerate person is able to glorify God and enjoy Him forever.[28]

---

28 In the Old Testament, the word for "glory" (kabod) means "weight"; in the New Testament the word for glory (doxa) means "fame" or "reputation." The two were brought together by the Apostle Paul in II Corinthians 4:17 where he wrote of the "weight of glory [doxa]." Thus the idea of glorifying God is to so give Him the proper recognition (or weight) in all things so that His fame (or good reputation) is spread widely among all men. The task of all Christians, and the task of those who help them, is possible to achieve only by people who have been regenerated.

For what, then, should the counselor who understands these things strive? First, he will never seek to counsel those he has insufficient reason to believe have been regenerated. But how can he know one way or the other? We must face the fact that he cannot know absolutely. God has not granted us the ability to look into one another's heart. In I Samuel 16:8 we read, "Man looks at the outward appearance, but the LORD looks at the heart." We do not know for sure whether or not anyone who seeks counsel has a heart of stone or flesh. God has granted us the ability to judge only his words and works. Therefore, we judge on the basis of what has been called "a credible profession of faith." That is, a profession of faith in which, after careful examination of his life and his testimony, the elders of a Bible-believing church have been satisfied sufficiently to receive him into communicant membership in their congregation. Even then, of course, there may be misjudgments.[29] Like a Pharisee, people may pretend, and their pretense may deceive for a time. Credible membership in the church, however, is the fundamental requirement for counseling.[30]

Second, if there is sufficient doubt about a would-be counselee's regeneration, then (because of the external evidence) the counselor should refuse to counsel. He should say something like the following: "I am glad that you came for help. After listening to some of your problems, I am happy to tell you that God has solutions to every one of them. There is, however, one difficulty. The solutions of which I speak are available only to God's children. Not everyone is a child of God. If you have never become His child, then you must do so before I can counsel you. In John 1:11 and 12, He says, 'He [Jesus Christ] came to His own creation, and

---

29 The Personal Data Inventory, a sample of which may be found in The Christian Counselor's Manual, has a section that is designed to help you evaluate whether or not one is a Christian. Copies of the PDI may be duplicated for use without asking for permission.

30 Apart from conclusive testimony, a counselor does not independently judge the member of such a church unregenerate.

His own people didn't receive Him. But to as many as did receive Him He gave the right to become God's children; to those who believe in His Name.' You see, God says one must 'become' His child by 'believing.' Let me explain...." And so the counselor, for the time being, steps out of his counseling role and into the role of an evangelist, only to resume the former role if and when the "counselee" professes faith in Christ and unites with the church.

It is fruitless to attempt to counsel unregenerate persons. They cannot and will not receive the things of God and His Word (I Corinthians 2:14). And it is harmful to attempt to do so. The unregenerate "counselee" may do as you direct him, but it will not last because what he does will be done outwardly, and there will be no inward reality to sustain it. Then when it all comes apart, the person "counseled" will think that God's way (as he interprets it) failed! Jesus spoke of the Pharisees who, like a cup washed only on the outside, nevertheless were dirty within. We don't need new Pharisees in the church! There are plenty of them already without creating them in "counseling" sessions.

So it is important, so far as one is able to discern, to counsel only regenerate persons. If over and over again in counseling, a person who is a member of a fine church such as I have described above fails to do as God requires in His Word because he is unable to understand or do it, there may be reason to question his regeneration. In such cases, the matter, if not remedied in counseling itself, ought to be brought before the elders of his church.

So regeneration, the power of God to transform corrupt natures so as to enable individuals to begin replacing old thoughts and old ways with their biblical alternatives, is absolutely essential to proper counseling. Unlike so many well-meaning but foolish counselors who will counsel anyone, I urge you to take care about this matter and, in the end, settle for nothing less than dealing with regenerate persons.

One other implication that I wish to draw from the biblical doctrine of regeneration or quickening is that because the change is brought about by the Spirit of God – and not by the person regenerated – there is every reason to have hope in counseling. The Spirit does not begin a work that He fails to complete: "He Who began a good work among you will keep on perfecting it until the Day of Christ Jesus" (Philippians 1:6). The Spirit dwells within the believer for the very purpose of perfecting his work, with a view to presenting the believer complete in Christ. I shall have more to say about this as we continue.

Chapter Four
How is Sanctification Effected?

We have seen that man is wholly passive in the act of regeneration; he contributes nothing to it. God alone effects it by His Spirit. One who is "*dead* in trespasses and sins" cannot give life to himself. He cannot raise himself from the dead. He cannot *create* himself anew. He cannot *give birth* to himself. All such things,[31] if and when they occur, must be brought about by an external Force. The scriptural figures of speech – birth, resurrection, creation – powerfully speak to this fact. The idea that faith regenerates is absurd on the face of it. The uncreated, the dead, and the unborn can do nothing – not even exercise faith. As a matter of fact, the Scriptures teach that faith itself, which is a *product* of regeneration (or quickening), is a *gift* (Ephesians 2:8, 9). A gift is something that another presents to you. It is neither earned by nor provided by oneself.

So regeneration is an act of God, performed solely by Him upon those to whom He determines to show His love. But is sanctification, which regeneration makes possible, *like* regeneration in this respect? As in regeneration, is the believer passive during the process of sanctification? The answer is, "Most certainly not!" Regeneration – the imparting of life, giving birth, creating anew

---
31 These are the three principal images or figures of speech under which regeneration is set forth in Scripture. All three, in one way or another, speak of imparting life or "quickening."

– is described by expressions that also indicate that once one gets on the lee side of regeneration, the now regenerate Christian surely will become active. Life implies growth and all of the activities that encourage it. Resurrection implies newness of life-style that will take the place of the old one. Creation implies fresh outlooks, responsibilities, and endeavors! All three terms imply purposes to achieve. There is a reason for regeneration! Why should there be such changes in the believer if there is nothing for him to do with the new orientation and capabilities that he has received? It simply doesn't compute.

Despite views that teach otherwise, the Bible sets forth sanctification as a process (not an act) in which three forces, the Spirit, His Word, and the regenerated saint, all *work together* to bring about change. It is vital to understand this essential fact and to keep all three of these forces in a harmonious and complementary relationship. None of them must be pitted against the others, as some who hold other views often do. Rather, it must be understood that every attempt to eliminate or minimize one or more of the three leads to failure in living and in counseling. It is precisely *because* of the tight interrelationship of the three elements in sanctification that the counselor gets involved. He helps the Christian to bring into play all three elements so that the process moves forward as God intended. The counselor, therefore, must understand each of the parts played in the process of sanctification by the Spirit, the Word, and the believer.

Obviously, the biblical counselor is not involved in the act of regeneration, in which the Spirit alone transforms the person. But now that the person has been transformed, his new orientation (toward God and righteousness) and his new capacity (to think and do those things that please God) bring that new person himself prominently into the picture. He must use the new ways of thinking and living that regeneration has made possible for God's glory. They must not be allowed to lie dormant. It is the counselor's task, among others, to help the counselee to recognize, understand, and draw upon the new resources that he possesses. One of the major reasons some counseling falls short is the failure of the believer to understand, call upon, and integrate all the resources that God has provided for him to encounter, fight, and defeat sin in his life.

Counselors and counselees must reject every form of "quietism," both because of its unbiblical nature and because of the frustration and defeat it occasions.[32] Often connected with quietism is the concept of a "second work of grace," the "baptism (or filling) of the Spirit" or a "second blessing." These and other names are used to describe an instantaneous act of God at some point subsequent to regeneration,[33] by which the believer is raised to a "higher plane." The way into this seemingly glorious, cloud

---

32 Quietistic teachings all stress change through human passivity. The pursuit of holiness through active obedience to Scripture is often derisively labeled "activism," and Christians are carefully steered away from it. Rather, a quietistic formula (they do not all agree) is offered instead. Quietistic "techniques" for change consist primarily in "letting go and letting God," as some have expressed it. The idea is that the more the Christian does, the more harm he will do and the less he will grow. To the extent to which he becomes actively involved in his sanctification, it will fail. This, we are told, is because self is the problem. Every effort by the self – even the transformed self – must be rejected and eschewed. Instead, the believer must let God effect change for him, instead of him. This passive approach, in effect, denies the transforming work of the Spirit in regeneration, or at best makes it pointless. If regeneration accomplishes any transformation at all, it is merely to open the believer to the further work of the Spirit. It is only as he "rests," "abides," or depends more and more on God to do what he cannot (and must not attempt) that he is sanctified. Biblical teaching, however, stresses the renewal of the believer in such a way that he may actually please God by what he thinks and does. His new abilities and capacities are to be used, not avoided.

33 Although some believe that it may happen concomitant with regeneration.

nine experience differs according to each system. The Christian may be instructed to follow a prescribed set of steps. Or he may be informed that it is by yielding, or by making a total[34] consecration, that instantaneous or entire sanctification will take place. The result of taking this action (or commitment to inaction), we are told, is either to attain to a state where one may have greater "victories" over temptation and sin, or to attain to "entire sanctification." The latter "result" may be presented either as a total eradication of sin or as an ability to do everything in "perfect love."[35] "Mistakes"[36] are still thought to be made, or it is taught that all willful sin is eradicated (inadvertent sin, it seems, does not count). Sometimes, in spite of the perfectionism involved in such teaching, the need for growth is postulated. But such growth is usually not thought

---

34 Avoid any belief that requires total or absolute "surrender" (or some similar term; see also Andrew Murray's book entitled Absolute Surrender). The fallacy of a system that teaches the need for this sort of experience is that total freedom from sin or its power supposedly is the result of total "yielding." This is begging the question. If the system were consistent, its adherents would declare a total commitment to be impossible until one had already attained perfection (that is, total sinlessness). But then, of course, commitment leading toward sanctification would not be needed! The fact is, since no believer is free from sin (I John 1:8), a total commitment (the phrase used by Charles Solomon and others) is impossible. James 3:2, 8, states, "All of us stumble in many ways. If any body doesn't stumble in speech, he is a perfect man... but no human being anywhere is able to tame the tongue." While one may make progress in bridling the tongue, the problem of an unruly tongue (as well as the many other ways in which James says we all stumble) is a problem we shall face so long as we are in this present body.

35 John Wesley's terminology for sinlessness.

36 Sins are either toned down and called "mistakes," or the list and type of sins is shrunk to those of an easily "avoidable" nature and number. Either way, in order to justify this view, the lifestyle is viewed as free from sin by greatly minimizing sin. In helping those who shorten the list of sins, counselors will have to emphasize that a sin is doing what God forbids and/or failing to do what He requires.

of in terms of the putting off/putting on dynamic of Colossians 3 and Ephesians 4, where *sinful living* is *being replaced* daily by righteousness living. On the whole, there is a wide range of similar beliefs that fall into the same basic scheme of quietistic and/or instantaneous sanctification, which differ only in minor details. But regardless of how these details differ, they have one thing in common: for them, sanctification is not a matter of on-going struggle, active pursuit, obedience, or growth; rather, it comes in some other way – usually in some crisis experience.

In these beliefs, passages having to do with our *status* before God that refer to what John Murray called "definitive sanctification" (the setting aside of a person to God at the time of justification) are wrongly applied to the post-regenerate, post-justified believer. As I have indicated previously, this status before God serves as the goal toward which our daily sanctification is to progressively move.[37] Definitive and progressive sanctification – what is on the record and what must be done to live up to that record – are obviously closely associated, but it is an error to equate rather than distinguish them. Definitive sanctification verses declare that "in Christ," by God's act, we have been set apart to Him as His "saints." We do not go on daily becoming saints. But we must work at becoming saintly. Even the failing, sinning Christians in Corinth are called "saints" because they were by God's act set apart from others as His people. In such passages, the word "sanctified" is used in a sense nearly identical to "justified."[38] Passages referring to progressive sanctification, on the other hand, refer to struggle, growth, and the pursuit and attainment of more and more holiness in daily living.

This book is principally concerned with progressive sanctification. We have seen that there are three elements that

---

37 See also Colossians 3:1–9, where considering oneself raised into heaven "together with Christ" is used as an incentive to holy living!
38 I am not saying that the words *mean* the same thing, but that, from different approaches, they refer to the same thing.

combine to bring about more and more holiness in the regenerated believer. The *Spirit* uses His *Word* as He enables the *believer* in faith and practice to obey it. It is each of these three elements that we now must consider in turn.

Chapter Five

The Spirit, Sanctification, and Counseling

What the Spirit of holiness[39] begins, He continues and (ultimately) completes.[40] But it is that period between the beginnings of holiness and the believer's perfection that we shall consider in this chapter.

Peter unequivocally says to his readers that you were "chosen according to the foreknowledge of God the Father, that *by the Spirit's sanctification* you may obey…" (I Peter 1:2, emphasis mine). Here, God's electing intention for the believer is obedient living.[41] And it is "by"[42] the sanctification that the Spirit produces that one "obeys" God's commands. That one verse contains all three of the

---

39 Romans 1:4. The phrase "Spirit of holiness" means "the Spirit from Whom holiness comes," and shows the absolute necessity of the Spirit's work not only in regeneration but also subsequent to it in sanctifying those He regenerates.
40 The spirits of just (justified) men are "made perfect" (complete) in glorification, Hebrews 12:23. Obviously, the context (Hebrews 12:22, 23) makes it clear that men are made perfect in (and not before) the "heavenly Jerusalem."
41 See also Ephesians 2:10, where Paul says that God's attention for Christians is to "create" them "for good works."
42 That is, "by" in the sense of "by means of." Here, the Greek *en* is used instrumentally.

elements that we mentioned at the close of the previous chapter: the Spirit, the Word (the only place where the will of God that must be obeyed can be found)[43], and the regenerate believer (who does the obeying). But notice the "setting apart" (or sanctification) is said to be the Spirit's" sanctification. He is the one Who primarily produces it. It is therefore rightly called "His."

He is the One Who "carried along" the writers of Scripture, so that what they wrote was, at the same time, precisely what God wanted them to say and what they themselves wanted to say. The words of the Bible can be called the Spirit's speech (as the writer of Hebrews calls them in passages such as Hebrews 3:7; 10:15, 16). So, the Spirit brings about sanctification by providing the Standard (the Bible) by which progress in holy living may be judged. And according to I Corinthians 2:9 through 12, it is the Spirit Who opens the eyes and the ears of the regenerate believer to understand that Word. Such matters are incomprehensible (even "foolishness;" I Corinthians 1:18) to "modern-day leaders" of the world who do not have the Spirit within them (I Corinthians 2:8). Moreover, God has poured the Spirit into our hearts (Romans 5:5) in order to motivate us by the love that is "producing in us what pleases Him" (Hebrews 13:21).[44] It is by the Spirit that the "new person" in Christ is being renewed in such a way as to produce the "full knowledge that is in keeping with the image of his Creator." (Colossians 3:10).

What is it that the Spirit is doing to renew us? God the Father is *enabling* the regenerate believer to "walk by the Spirit" as He fights

---

43 For an in-depth treatment of this assertion, see my book *The Christian's Guide to Guidance*.

44 See also Philippians 2:13. God is working "in us" through the Spirit, Who dwells within us. When we were baptized with the Spirit (I Corinthians 12:13) at regeneration, He took up residence in us for the purpose of equipping us "with every good thing for doing His will" (Hebrews 13:21a).

against the "desires of the flesh" (Galatians 5:16).[45] And He does this by *replacing* the works of the flesh (Galatians 5:19–21) with His "fruit" (Galatians 5:22– 24). Paul's argument is that, having been granted newness of life "by the Spirit," we should also "walk by the Spirit" (Galatians 5:25).[46] To walk by the Spirit means to live according to His Word, His wisdom, and His power.

How does the Spirit help Christians to do this? By "renewing" (literally, "rejuvenating," Ephesians 4:23) them in "the attitude" of their "minds." This new orientation, as we have called it earlier in this book, has to do with one's *attitude* toward God and righteousness as well as his attitude toward himself and his own thoughts and ways. The attitude previous to regeneration and the reception of the Holy Spirit is toward one's own desires, ideas, and ways, while it is *away from God, His thoughts, and His ways.* The new "attitude of mind" is *toward God and His righteousness.* This changed "attitude" and ability to comprehend God's Word enables one who has been "created" anew "in God's likeness with righteousness and holiness that come from the truth," to "put off lying…" and so forth (Ephesians 4:24–25). The Spirit works through, not apart from, the new attitudes and capacities of the regenerate believer. That is one reason for "renewing" him.

---

45 Paul is speaking about the habits and patterns of thinking and doing developed before regeneration that are brought over into the postregenerate life. These habits desire to continue and to gain ascendancy in the new life. For details about this problem and the Spirit's solution to it, see my discussion of "flesh" in Romans 6 and 7 found in *Winning the War Within*.

46 Because we have "crucified the flesh with its passions and desires" *by the Spirit* in definitive sanctification ("If we live [have been brought to spiritual life] by the Spirit;" Galatians 5:25), we are to "walk" by the Spirit in daily life (progressive sanctification). See Jesus' call to discipleship in which we are called to "take up the cross" (i.e., to crucify "the desires of the flesh" as we "deny" our own desires; Matthew 16:24).

The new "attitude" toward *truth* that the Spirit has created in the regenerated believer is a craving to learn and to do what God says in His Word. It is clear that sanctification takes place through a "knowledge of the truth" (cf. John 17:17: "Sanctify them by Your truth; Your Word is truth," NKJV). Notice, also, that "the new person" is being "renewed in such a way as to produce full knowledge that is in keeping with the image of his Creator" (Colossians 3:10). According to Ephesians 4:24, the "new person" is "created in God's likeness with righteousness and holiness [sanctification] that *come from the truth*" (emphasis mine). Once again, it is the Spirit Who provides and Who enables one to believe and follow the "truth." It is He who progressively sanctifies the person as he comprehends truth and lives it in accordance with Titus 1:1 where Paul writes that "the full knowledge of the truth …is in the interest of godliness." In other words, the two-fold problem set forth by Isaiah (55:8, 9) is being solved by the Spirit through the Word that He inspired. The Spirit revealed the truth of the Word (I John 2:27) and, as believers study and apply it in life, the Spirit inculcates its teachings in their attitudes, minds, and walk. According to I John 4:6 and 5:7, the Spirit is called "the Spirit of truth." Because of the Spirit's presence and work in us (I John 4:13) we are said to be "of the truth" (I John 3:19) and are urged to love not only by word, but also by "deed and truth." So it is "the teachings of God's Spirit" (in Scripture) that Christians are able to "investigate spiritually" – that is, by the Spirit Who dwells within (I Corinthians 2:14).

Now, of course, it is possible for Christians to behave "like fleshly people" (I Corinthians 3:3). What does that mean? He is speaking about believers who, because they fail to appropriate their resources as they should (see also Philippians 4:19), are "walking like men without the Spirit" (I Corinthians 3:3). In other words, believers ought to be walking in accordance with God's will because they are men *with* the Spirit! That is to say, when relying on His

Word and following it by His power, they have the knowledge and the ability to walk in His will.

So Paul's prayer for the Colossians is that they "may be filled with the full knowledge of His [God's] will in all spiritual wisdom and understanding" (Colossians 1:9). *Spiritual* wisdom and understanding is the wisdom and understanding that the Spirit provided in the Bible and that He enables believers to understand and live by. This wisdom and understanding were provided not simply to "fill" their heads, but also to enable them "to walk in a way that is worthy of the Lord, pleasing him in everything" (Colossians 1:10). And he continued, praying that they "be empowered with every sort of power" to do so (v. 11).

At the conclusion of that first chapter of Colossians, Paul sums up everything in this passage concerning the ministry of the Word by saying, "which is Christ in you, the hope of glory, Whom we announce, counseling every person and teaching every person as wisely as possible" (Colossians 1:28). This leads us now to turn to the human element in the matter (that of the counselee and the counselor).

Chapter Six

The Human Factor in Sanctification

Some years ago I was invited to speak at a Keswick conference in Trinidad. Halfway through the conference the leaders drew me aside to talk. They said, in effect, "What you are teaching is different from what we have heard before. You are saying that we can *do* something about our problems." They were amazed at the notion and pleasantly relieved that they did not have to sit by, idly "resting" or incessantly "yielding," while waiting for God to do something in them and for them. They misunderstood Romans 12:1:

> I urge you then, brothers, because of these mercies from God, to present your bodies as living, holy, pleasing sacrifices to God, which is the reasonable way to serve Him in worship.

They had been taught that "yielding" (or "presenting") one's body meant surrendering it to God to do as He pleased with it, and that, as a result, they would not have to do anything themselves. God would give them a higher life as the result of "presenting" (or yielding). It had not worked, they told me, and they were surprised to discover (as I showed them) that Romans 1:1 was but an echo of Romans 6:13 through 19, where the expressions "present your bodily members" (v. 13), "present yourselves" (v. 16) and "present your members" (v. 19) first occur. I went on to make the point that in these passages in Romans 6, the bodily members were to be presented "as instruments of righteousness" to be used in "obedience" as God's slaves who are "to bring about sanctification" (v. 13, 16, 19). In other words, God expected them to use their bodies to serve Him in His righteous ways, thereby also bringing about their "sanctification" and its "fruit" (v. 22).

This passage pictures someone who had been a slave to sin, obeying its commands and thereby using the members of his body to further unrighteousness, switching allegiance to God as his new Master. Just as he had used his body in the service of sin, he is now to use it in the service of God and righteousness. Surely before conversion he did not "rest" or "yield" to sin in some quietistic manner! Nothing of the sort was in Paul's mind. Nor did anything like it flow from his pen. The Christian is to present himself to God as His slave who is willing to "obey from the heart the pattern of teaching to which he was handed over" (v. 17). His task is now "to bring about sanctification" as he once brought about "lawlessness" (v. 19). There is nothing but activity, service, and obedience in the passage!

So there is a part that the believer must play in his sanctification. That is clear. Indeed, if there were nothing he could do, if he had no part, counseling would be useless. All one could do, were this the case, would be to urge the Christian who is in trouble to yield again – this time more completely or more sincerely. And when this failed, as indeed it would, the message to him would be the same! After a while, as these Trinidadian believers discovered, their hopes would flag; their discouragements would mount. They would soon adopt one of two attitudes: they would say "What's the use?" Or, on the other hand, in self-deceit, they might pretend to themselves (and perhaps to others) that they were living life "on a higher plane."

Every biblical counselor must recognize that his message should be quite different from that of the quietist. While he will in no way diminish the emphasis upon the necessary work of the Spirit that I have highlighted in the previous chapter, neither will he play down the part of the counselee himself. Everywhere in Scripture, the Christian is commanded to obey God's Word. To intimate that he may do so apart from the Spirit and the Word is the serious error that the quietist thinks we fall into. And indeed, if any of us call upon a counselee to struggle with his problems in his own wisdom and power, we certainly fall into the error of which the quietists accuse us. But that is not the teaching of those who belong to the nouthetic movement because that is not the teaching of the Bible.

Now, contrary to the quietist's ideas of our counseling, we teach that counselees should be confronted with the commands of God's Word and called upon to obey them (Matthew 28:20) "from the heart"[47] (Romans 6:17) *by the enabling power* of the Spirit *according to*, and never *apart from*, the Bible. Thus all three elements in sanctification are to be brought into play in biblical counseling.

I will not take the time here to develop this point further, since in my book *The Theology of Counseling*, chapter fifteen,[48] I have discussed in depth the believer's "Pursuit of Fruit," which is encouraged in I Timothy 6:11 and II Timothy 2:22. The interesting thing is that while in Galatians 5 Paul stresses that fruit is the result of the Spirit's work, in these two passages in the pastorals he stresses the part that the Christian plays in pursuing it. Neither passage is to be used to the exclusion of the other. In one context, the need to emphasize dependence on the Spirit may be paramount; in others, there will be a need to stress responsibility. But one must be careful never to give the impression that what is said is all there is

---

47 That is, genuinely, as whole persons; not by pharisaical, outward conforming.

48 See also my book *Maintaining the Delicate Balance in Christian Living*, where I discuss the need for the biblical balance between human and the divine elements.

to the story. Paul never did. He was able to say both that the Spirit produces the fruit and that the Christian himself must pursue it – without contradiction.

That there is abundant biblical data on this point is clear. There is no commandment given to the Holy Spirit (or to "Christ in us"); all commands are given to the Christian. It is he, not anyone else, who must obey. You will find Christians who have been taught that the Spirit (or Christ in them) will do everything if they simply yield. If they are still confused after hearing an explanation of the biblical teaching, you might give them the following homework assignment, which I have found helpful in such cases. Send them home to go through the book of I Corinthians (or any fairly long New Testament book) noting on paper every time the Holy Spirit (or Christ in you) is commanded to do something and every time that the believer is commanded to do something. When they return with no notes about verses that command the Spirit or Christ to do anything and notes that show every command is given to the believer, it helps to drive home your point.

It is important, then, to develop from the Bible the doctrine of human responsibility for sanctification. But always make it clear that part of that responsibility is to call upon God for the wisdom and strength to obey (as Paul did in Colossians 1:9–14). These two qualities come from the Spirit using His Word – to which subject we now must turn our attention.

Chapter Seven

Sanctification and the Word

Jesus' words, "Sanctify them by the truth; Your Word is truth" (John 17:17) say it all. Yet it seems some have difficulty believing it. Sanctification does not take place apart from the Word of God, the Bible. There is no hope of spiritual growth for those who depend on hunches, promptings and checks in the spirit, feelings, and the like. Because I have dealt with this matter in *The Christian's Guide to Guidance*, I shall do little more here than to note the danger of turning outside of the Word of God to such supposed means of instruction in solving counseling problems. The emphasis on subjective, experience-oriented teaching always leads astray.

But let me ask one question: When God has provided such clear-cut direction in His Word, why is it that Christians ignore it and turn to other supposed sources of help? We should be so delighted to think that God has provided this inerrant guide to life and godliness that we ought to spend as much time as we can delving into it. Think of it: the living God, the Creator, and Sustainer of all things, has condescended not only to send His Son to die for our sins to save us but also to give Christians a wonderful Book with all that we need to serve and love Him and our neighbors (See also II Peter 1:3; II Timothy 3:17)! What foolishness, not to say ingratitude, on the part of those who fail to obtain the help that God has provided and that they need, and as a result, lead miserable lives, hurt His cause, and disgrace His Name – all because they neglect to study and appropriate the truths of the Bible! It is almost unthinkable!

Counselors, if you fail to stress the utter importance of the Scriptures as the third element in furthering the process of sanctification, you are equally remiss. There is no excuse to allow (not to mention encourage) counselees to turn anywhere else for help in sanctification. When you detect a dependence by counselees upon outside sources of "help," it is your duty to help them to see that this is one, if not the principal, reason that they have gotten into trouble. Your task, in such cases, is not only to help them straighten out the presenting problem, but also to help them with the greater problem – their failure to use Scripture to frame their lives. Having helped a counselee out of his difficulty, it is then worthwhile to take an extra session or two to discuss the whole matter of God's Standard for faith and practice – the Bible – and how to get help from it.

Obviously, you do not have time to teach a course on biblical interpretation, application, and implementation in counseling sessions, but you ought to take the time to strongly urge them to learn all they can about such matters. It was because of these time limitations despite the need for such study that I wrote the book *What to Do on Thursday*. This book not only takes the reader through a course in interpretation, application, and implementation but also does so in a unique way. It does not simply set forth abstract principles without showing the reader how to move from the problem to the biblical solutions. Rather, it starts with the problem (encountered on Thursday – or any other day) and leads to the Bible, showing how to locate, interpret, and use the passages that are pertinent to the problem. If you do not have some better way of helping counselees to "get into" the Scriptures in a similar or better way, I urge you to examine this volume to see whether or not it is exactly what you need to give to counselees. At any rate, it is necessary to help counselees learn how to use the Bible to solve problems, or they will be back in the counseling room in six months or sooner!

All that I have said about turning to supposed "help" from outside of the Bible so far applies every bit as much to those counselors and counselees who believe that the principles and practices of pagan counselors can aid in the sanctifying process. I have already noted John 17:17 at the head of this chapter. In that verse we are told that it is truth that sanctifies. But notice, the source of truth is said to be God's Word.

God spoke His Word audibly and in dreams and visions in times past, and He sent His Son Jesus Christ as the embodiment of that Word (Hebrews 1:1–3; John 1:1). But the revelation of truth which He has given to us was completed with the writing of the last book of the New Testament.[49] And the revelation of every other sort mentioned above is dependent upon what He has revealed about it in the Scriptures. So our one source of special revelation is the Bible. Every counselor must come to this conviction and counsel in the light of it or he should stop calling himself a "biblical" counselor.

In spite of what I have just said, there are those who seek to integrate biblical truth with the fallible theories and the ideas of men. That is sad, not to say harmful. When God's pristine, perfect truth is diluted by the addition of the pagan ideas of men, whose thoughts are not God's thoughts and whose ways are not His (remember Isaiah 55:8, 9), the "help" that is offered is seriously weakened. Often the "help" is no help at all. We find so-called "biblical" counselors reasoning from human wisdom about how God will permit divorce for reasons not given in the Bible. We find them offering advice about child rearing that is contrary to what God teaches. We find counselors excusing counselees from responsibility for sinful behavior because of their upbringing. And

---

49 I have dealt with the cessation of special revelation in my book *Signs and Wonders in the Last Days* (q.v.).

the list of aberrations from biblical truth go on and on. It is time to stop this! Are you one who has been unfaithful to God's Word, seeking to find truth elsewhere?

Now, don't tell me that "all truth is God's truth." That old weary argument is threadbare. Everyone agrees about that slogan. But the corollary is that "all error is the devil's error." How can you tell which is which? Obviously, there must be a standard by which truth can be discerned. The Bible itself is that Standard. So it turns out that all paths lead the Christian back to the Bible.

But equally telling is the fact that God's special revelation – revelation about life and godliness – is revealed only in the Bible. There the Christian counselor can find "*all things* necessary for life and godliness" (II Peter 1:3–6 [emphasis mine]). And, according to that passage, the things that make the believer's life "active"[50] and "fruitful" (v. 8) are the biblical "promises" of God through which one may become a "partaker of the divine [i.e., divinely-given] nature" (v. 4) that enables him to escape from "the corruption that is in the world." In other words, these promises separate one from it, or, we may say, sanctify him. He must "make every effort" to bring the qualities mentioned in the passage into his life (v. 5).

In his letters, the Apostle John warns about the many false teachers who seek to lead Christians astray. In discussing this matter in his letter to the "elect lady," he wrote,

> Watch yourselves, that you don't lose that which you have worked for, but rather that you may receive a full reward. Everybody who goes beyond, and doesn't remain in the teaching of Christ, doesn't have God. The one who remains in the teaching has both the Father and the Son (II John 8, 9).

Now, there are several facts to note in that statement. First, there are those who would lead Christians away from what the

---

50 N.B., quietistically-inclined counselor!

Sanctification and the Word

apostles taught about Christ. That temptation has continued until today. Second, those Christians who were advancing in sanctification by "working" for it could lose something of the "reward" they might otherwise have had by succumbing to the temptation to "go beyond" the apostolic message. Note, incidentally, the "active" human element that John says is involved! Third, these false teachings came from people who did not "have God" as Father and Son. Fourth, the one who remains in apostolic teaching (which today is found only in the Bible) demonstrates by his continuing fidelity to the teaching that he "has both the Father and the Son." Finally, the problem is stated in these terms: the temptation is to "go beyond."

Go beyond what? The text makes that clear: the temptation is to "go beyond" the "teaching" (v. 9). It is interesting that the one who goes beyond is viewed as no longer "remaining" in the apostolic teaching (now found in the New Testament). It is not a matter of simply *diluting* by adding to, but a matter of *abandoning* by going beyond. Every counselor who turns to the theories of ungodly psychologists and other counselors places himself in the position of going beyond the biblical teaching about life and godliness. If he allows his counselees to seek counsel outside Scripture, he fails to warn them as John did.

In either case, there is the possibility of losing one's reward. Rather, the counselor should aim at the "full reward" for both himself and his counselees. To play around with the theories of men, rather than adhere to the truth of God, is to place oneself and one's counselees in the way of serious danger. John is quite strong on this point: "Everybody who goes beyond, and doesn't remain in the teaching of Christ, *doesn't have God*" (emphasis mine). It may be that some of those in the church calling themselves "Christian counselors" who "go beyond" the truths of the Bible that are designed to sanctify are not truly Christians at all. I have known those who began to do what they called Christian counseling who, after dabbling in all sorts of beliefs other than the Bible, became enamored with them, left the Bible behind, and became full-fledged non-Christian counselors. They now make no pretense about being "biblical" or "Christian" in their counseling. Counselor, are you tempted to adopt non-Christian teachings? Counselee, does the counselor from whom you seek help take his directions from the Bible? Or does he "go beyond"?

There are many other passages to which we might turn in showing how the Bible, along with the Spirit and the counselee himself, all play a part in sanctification. Remember, each must be given its proper due. To state it simply, the counselor must urge the counselee to think and do what God, in Scripture, says he ought to, by the power of the Spirit working through the Word to inform and enable him through prayer. At every point, the counselor should set the example of these things for his counselee. Then, and then alone, will you see people growing by grace (II Peter 3:18).

Chapter Eight

Let's Talk about Counseling

So far, I have spent the lion's share of the space in this book discussing sanctification. That was important since it was necessary to establish clearly what we are talking about. I have mentioned counseling largely in an incidental way. It is time to zero in on some of the major issues in counseling that are related to sanctification.

I want to spell out again, from a different angle, two reasons that a thorough understanding of sanctification and its place in counseling should be of importance to counselors. First, counseling usually begins when the process of sanctification comes to a halt or is seriously impeded by some problem. In such times, counseling is specifically intended to assist the progress of sanctification. That is why counseling comes into play. Second, the matters with which counselors are concerned in counseling are sanctification matters. For these reasons, the counselor should not be indifferent to issues having to do with Christian growth. Because both of these issues are of such great importance, I intend to devote a chapter to each.

To begin with, an individual usually needs counseling because of some factor that has blocked the normal growth process. It is then that he seeks help from a counselor or others urge him to do so. Often, it is a wife who urges her husband to go to counseling with her; less frequently it is the other way around. Sometimes some interested party such as a parent, a child, a relative, or a friend encourages counseling. And then there are institutional influences – a Christian school or some other organization may insist on counseling for a student or a worker. And last but certainly not least, a pastor may initiate the process by going to the person or persons involved and offering his services.

These persons, and perhaps others as well, advise people to seek counseling because they detect something wrong about the attitudes, the words, or the behaviors of the one whom they encourage to receive counseling. In effect, though they may not put it in these terms, they perceive that their Christian brother or sister has stopped growing, that the process of sanctification in one way or another is stymied. They may see a marriage that is faltering. They may sense an attitude of depression, defeat, or dismay. They may encounter a brother who has ceased using the means of grace (Bible study, prayer, church attendance, etc.). They may catch another in sin (Galatians 6:1); they may suspect that there is a problem of some sort and, having confronted the person, discover that they were right. All of this ought to be done out of loving concern (though, sadly, that does not always happen). But each of these reasons for encouraging someone to seek counsel is based on the idea (not always understood or expressed as such) that the person has ceased growing in his Christian life as he should. That is to say, the process of sanctification has come to a halt or has been greatly set back.

So we see that sanctification is the counselor's biblical, immediate concern. The counselor should, from the very start, consider his counselee's situation and problem differently than the non-Christian or integrationist counselor. He should always be thinking about counseling problems *in terms of sanctification.*

What does that mean? Among other things, it means that he will want to know about the counselee's growth patterns prior to the onset of the problem(s). He will want to know how the counselee

Let's Talk about Counseling

views his problem – does he see it merely as a sad thing, a tragedy, a difficulty to be overcome, or a matter to be settled with others? Or does he see it as a setback in his growth by grace in serving and honoring God? That is to say, does he think of the problem in terms of sanctification or not? The counselor is concerned about the way in which the counselee thinks because often, he must turn the counselee's thinking and behavior from other concerns to focus on sanctification. Until both the counselor and the counselee think in those terms, the counseling will have a wrong focus and will go nowhere, at least as far as biblical growth out of sin and into righteousness is concerned.

The counselor will be concerned to discover two things: how these problems impede the process of sanctification and what measures must be taken to get the individual on the sanctification track once again. It is this orientation toward sanctification that makes biblical counseling unique. Other counselors do not think in those terms. Christian counselors, when counseling properly, always do. Their concern is not about counseling *per se*, it is not a concern with problems or even extricating counselees from them; rather, it is a concern about turning the counselee's thinking and ways from sin and toward righteousness.[51]

In this chapter, we are not so much interested in what to do about problems of sanctification as in asking how to think about what is wrong. The answer to that question could take many forms, but if sanctification is uppermost in the counselor's thinking, the many issues involved in understanding the counselee's problem will coalesce. That is not to say that complex matters will be oversimplified. But just as a farmer has a farming viewpoint to which he relates all else, so the counselor relates the many aspects of problems that emerge in data gathering[52] to this one issue: how

---

51 Remember Isaiah 55:8, 9!
52 For a two-chapter discussion of data gathering, see *The Christian Counselor's Manual*.

each aspect impinges upon sanctification. The importance of seeing the central place of sanctification in all that is done in counseling cannot be overstated. Sanctification is the thread that runs through all of counseling.

So, it is important to foster this outlook in one's counselees from the outset. Whenever a counselee wanders from the importance of pleasing God by spiritual growth on to some other trail, bring him back with words such as, "That may all be true, but how does what you are now talking about help you to grow and love God and your neighbor?" A believer ought to respond favorably to such interrogations, so long as he does not use them as a way of avoiding issues. The idea is not to distract the counselee's attention from something he considers important; rather, it is to help him to view the matter in different terms, in a different context. It is to help him to see that God is involved in the problem and that the manner of understanding and dealing with the problem must be one that reflects that fact. And specifically, it is to help him view every matter from the perspective of how he may grow in his spiritual life and thereby honor God. Sanctification becomes the skewer on which the counselee impales all his problems. It is to give him a handle on the problems so that he can deal with them in a biblical manner.

It ought to be plain to every Christian counselor that his task is made possible by maintaining this sanctification emphasis. He need not go off in all directions, wondering where to begin or end. Instead, because he can hang everything on the sanctification issue, he can more easily determine what to do both in data gathering and in seeking solutions to the problems that he discovers. Indeed, keeping an eye fixed firmly on the goal of resuming and furthering sanctification in a counselee turns counseling into a valuable ministry that accords with the ongoing ministry of Christ's church, rather than making it something that is done outside of the context of church discipleship. It fits!

Understanding and maintaining this perspective in counseling enables the counselor to see that counseling is nothing in itself. It is but a means to an end. The end is the sanctification of the counselee. The *raison d'etre* for counseling is that the normal process of sanctification has stalled. Therefore, counseling is but a measure that is taken in order to break open the logjam and set the logs floating on their proper course. It diminishes the idea of being a "counselor" in the professional sense of the word – as, indeed it should! Counseling is a ministry of the church in which both ruling and teaching elders are to engage formally and officially, and in which all other members of the congregation are to engage informally and unofficially. The elder is a counselor *among other things*. There is no such thing as a professional counselor in the church other than an elder, and that is not his sole work. It is but one aspect of it. So, counseling is diminished in the sense that it is but one of the many tasks in which those who perform other work are engaged. No one ought to hang out a shingle and set himself or herself up as a "professional" biblical counselor. Keeping the goal of sanctification in view helps counselors to remember this.

Chapter Nine

Common Territory

The close affinity between counseling and Christian living in general (and sanctification in particular) is natural. The two are concerned with and operate in common territory. The overlap of which I speak is natural, I say, because the materials of growth by grace and those of biblical counseling are the same. Problem solving, putting off the "old person" while putting on the new, and the pursuit of the Spirit's fruit, for instance, are common themes of both. Both may turn to I Peter 1:15 as their common mission statement: "Instead, as the One Who called you is holy, you yourselves must become holy in all your behavior." In short, the desire to be sanctified (separate) motivates both counseling and normal Christian living.

These common desires and goals are the reason non-Christian counseling cannot cut it. The materials used, as well as the concerns and the motivation of non-biblical counseling just cited, are foreign to the mission of the individual Christian and the Christian counselor. Indeed, non-Christian counselors strongly disapprove of sanctification since, when you boil it down to its essentials to desire to be sanctified is a desire to become *different* – to be separate from others. Many consider this taboo.

Moreover, the goal of non-Christian counselors is to help counselees live up to the norm, to fit in with society. But the norm is that which the non-Christian culture of the day declares to be desirable.[53] The prevailing view among people today is relativism; that is, permission to believe whatever it is that you may wish to believe – except, of course, Christian teaching. One stated reason for this is Christianity's exclusiveness. It cuts across relativism, condemning it out of hand. Christianity says that since there is but one God, we must know and serve Him His way; that there is no other. That got the apostles into trouble in their time. It was okay to add another god to your pantheon in Greco-Roman culture, but it was not okay to declare all other gods to be nothing more than idols. There is much the same attitude in our times.

So, for Christians to turn to non-Christian counselors (or Christians who counsel according to their values) is to opt, in one way or another, for a relativistic solution to problems; one in which the counselee is "helped" by the counselor to blend into the culture. But Christians cannot do this since their beliefs are antithetical to the ambient culture.

Why is this so? How is it that the Christian must run against his culture? It is not out of a wish to be contrary. He would certainly prefer not to run headlong into the values of others around him – if they were values that the Bible allows him to accept. But they are not. Once again, the problem is this: God says that His ways and His thoughts are not those of the culture (Isaiah 55:8, 9). So, in order to conform to God's ways and thoughts, the believer must reject the world's and accept God's.

I have said that Christian counseling is a part of the sanctification process: that the two occupy common ground. There are few cases that biblical counselors take on that do not, to some extent, involve the problem of breaking up logjams. I have briefly referred to this elsewhere. The problem is that the stream of

---

53 See, for instance, Glasser, whose counseling expressly states that the goal is to make people fit in with whatever the prevailing culture may be.

sanctification has been clogged by unbiblical logs in the counselee's life. They must be broken up and sent downstream to the ocean. The reason logjams occur is that Christians do not always come for counseling help until serious jams have developed.[54]

The common territory occupied by Christian counseling and sanctification means that as the believer seeks to float away the unseemly aspects of his character, these in turn resist change. Breaking up logjams is what counselors do. By their counsel, they cause the normal flow of sanctification to resume.

Both the saint and his counselors, then, are different. No counselor but the Bible-believing one seeks to improve the progress of his counselee's sanctification. That's what true *Christian* (biblical) counseling is all about – making people different, God's way, shaping them in ways and thinking that does not fit their culture. When the Christian deserted the enemy and surrendered to God, he pledged to do His will and become like Him. He was given a new name and a new status. His basic outlook changed, he acquired new capacities; he received the Holy Spirit as his constant Companion and Helper. And now he is involved in the process of becoming more like Christ, into Whose stature the Spirit is shaping him. All of this was God's gracious doing.

It is amazing that God declares wretched, redeemed sinners His special people. They are different because He has chosen to sanctify and make them His own (I Peter 1:2).[55] But God now expects them to live up to their new name and status. His purpose is to make them holy (set apart) in fact as well as in standing. And

---

54 If they came earlier, much grief could be avoided and remedies would be simpler. Time complicates one's problem as more and more logs tend to pile up.

55 Peter tells his readers, "[You] are chosen according to the foreknowledge of God the Father, that by the Spirit's sanctification you may obey and be sprinkled by the blood of Jesus Christ." "Sprinkling" was a sacrificial means of purifying in which blood was sprinkled in order to sanctify.

that is where all the problems appear. Sanctification, which involves the process of clearing the stream of sin, *itself* may lead to logjams. Those logs that have been firmly lodged over the years may resist removal and become the occasion for more and more logs to pile up. When a Christian finds himself unable or unwilling to break them loose, counseling becomes necessary.

Many balk at the very idea of becoming different. Old logs of conformity refuse to budge. Christians may be happy to be labeled "saints" and to know that they are headed for heaven, but *becoming* a saint is something else. Sainthood means becoming different, and becoming different means standing out from the crowd. That takes courage. And courage is precisely what many Christians lack. Even the apostles prayed for boldness (Acts 4:29).

Right here is where the counselor may find that counselees cause the logjam. Counselees appreciate the benefits and privileges associated with sainthood, but they are often less than enamored with the consequences and responsibilities associated with it. A person who is *set apart* is *noticed* – every bit as much as the two words printed in italics in this sentence. Because his behavior is different, it becomes noticeable. Peter mentions this fact when he writes, "it surprises others that you won't run with them in the same ruinous excesses, and they insult you" (I Peter 4:4). Notice, particularly, the last clause: "and they insult you." There's the rub. Sainthood in the closet, sainthood away from the prying eyes of the disapproving crowd, is okay. But that it should be noticed. No thanks.

Indeed, because sainthood is noticed, Christians often find themselves ridiculed and challenged about their behavior. Then, too, they become obligated to "defend the hope that is in [them] to everybody who asks [them]" (I Peter 3:15). Many counselees would rather not. And in the following verse, notice especially that he tells his readers that they will be "slandered" by "those who speak insultingly about your good behavior in Christ" (v. 16). Slandered for good behavior! Think of it. That is where many stumble. Counselees may be willing to make cosmetic changes that are not too obvious – but real heart changes that lead to saintly behavior? Behavior that leads to insults? Well that's something else.

Christians get into trouble when they begin to live as they should and suffer consequences. Their number of close friendships may diminish. Since they live exclusive lives, they may find that others are more than happy to exclude them from theirs. They may find themselves becoming lonely, longing for companionship – especially if they neglect the fellowship of the church. They may become the butt of jokes, gossip, and slander. The more they conform to their name, *saints* ("the separated ones"), the more they become disassociated from those whose lifestyles they may not follow.

On the other hand, though a Christian rightly refuses to become a part of the "Christian elite" who try to encase themselves in protective coverings to isolate themselves from the world around them, nevertheless a believer's neighbors and business associates, even family members, may avoid him. In some cases, the latter may even disown him. He is different, and people don't like it! The Christian who lives as he ought to is not different for difference's sake. He is different because he is becoming more like His Lord!

In dealing with counselees who are bogged down by these considerations, counselors must take a lovingly firm stance. They will distinguish those counselees whose growth in grace has been stunted by discouragement and loneliness from those who have ceased growing out of fear. The first may have sought to become holy but didn't know how to find new friends after being abandoned by old ones. The second class may have ceased growing as the result of reversion to old ways through capitulating to the pressures exerted by those around them.

The first group needs to be brought to repentance over the lack of gratitude that has caused their dispirited attitude, while the latter need to repent and forsake their straying ways. Both the disheartened, lonely counselee and the straying sheep must be helped to become more closely associated with other believers in the church.

The first class needs the encouragement through fellowship that the church can provide. The second needs the emboldening that comes from stronger believers standing with them. Both need the stimulation to "love and good deeds" about which we read in Hebrews 10:24 and 25. In all of this, the idea is not to flee into the Christian bubble, isolating oneself from contact with the world, but to gain the strength and courage that enable a believer to live a consistent Christian witness before all men.

Counselors will take these matters to heart, and whenever they discover counselees who have become indolent or regressive will seek the correct response to their sin. They will help them appropriate the best resources in Christ and in His church. They will stress these resources since they recognize that they, themselves, cannot provide adequate assistance of the sort that the church surely can.[56]

Dealing with other sorts of problems, of course, will demand that counselors take appropriate measures. These problems, in addition to those just mentioned, also involve breaking up logjams and, in that respect, will not differ from those mentioned in other books (see *The Christian Counselor's Manual* and *How to Help People Change*). In speaking about breaking up logjams, I am not speaking of a specific sort of problem but rather of a problem that

---

56 The problem here is that not every church is ready to offer help. The counselor may have to work with members in the church as well as with his counselees in order to achieve this. Or, in the worst scenario, he may have to advise that a counselee leave his church and unite with another that will provide help.

may become a complicating factor when another problem is not quickly resolved. For help with logjams, see my book *Critical Stages of Biblical Counseling* in which I deal with the matter more fully.

For now, the important matter to understand is that unresolved problems curtail sanctification and therefore must be dealt with. Sanctification cannot continue unabated when there is unrepentant sin and unresolved problems in one's life. The counselee is a whole person, and a breakdown in one area of sanctification affects the whole of it. He cannot, for instance, go on knowingly lying about some matter without grieving the Holy Spirit Who provides the power for sanctification. And he will avoid the convicting efficacy of the Word and the preaching of the gospel as well. All of this leads to a setback of spiritual growth and sanctification. For this reason, the counselor must consider himself an agent in furthering the sanctification process. The territory is the same. When he understands this, he will add a dimension to his work that is unique among counselors by what he says and does in counseling. Truly Christian counseling, designed to assist in the counselee's sanctification, is unique. Clearly, the focus on sanctification in the counseling process is what makes it so.

Chapter Ten
Nouthetic Counseling Is Unique

At the conclusion of the previous chapter, I mentioned one unique feature of Christian (or nouthetic) counseling: it is part of the sanctification process. There are very few cases that counselors face that do not involve breaking up logjams, as we have seen. That is because counselees do not come soon enough, so the initial problem is compounded by other problems. But it also may be because counselees follow unbiblical counseling, which only adds to the logjam. This underscores the idea that true Christian counseling alone can help one grow by grace. Biblical counsel has several features that should be explained further:

❖ *A Unique Clientele.* Christian counselors have a unique clientele: they counsel only those who are capable of being sanctified. I discussed this earlier in the book. Because they are committed to following the premise that sanctification is (or ought to be) what we should achieve through counseling, they will not settle for doing anything else. They do not knowingly counsel unregenerate persons. Thus, the unique clientele grows out of the unique reason for counseling (not understood by others) – to further sanctification. But the same reason also leads to…

❖ *Unique Goals and Objectives.* All along the way, the counselor keeps biblical goals and objectives plainly in view. In addition to breaking logjams and permitting the process of sanctification to flow freely toward those goals and objectives, Christian counseling speeds up the process. It also focuses on helping counselees to avoid logjams in the future by adopting biblical lifestyles and pointing out areas in which sanctification has not yet begun or may be in danger of floundering. In examining his counselee's life, the counselor will often uncover such matters and can take preventive action that will help nip problems in the bud. In observing Christian counseling, one would also ascertain that

❖ *The Methods Are Unique.* For one thing, the counselor will pray and use his Bible. By introducing these elements into counseling, he gives recognition to the obvious fact that he is not dependent upon his own wisdom and ingenuity. He recognizes the presence of Another – with His supreme wisdom and power – in each counseling session. That unique fact in itself makes no small difference. Surely, it dramatically sets apart Christian counseling and its methods from all other counseling. In full accord with the fact of dependence on God and His Word, every method the believer employs in the course of counseling should grow out and be appropriate to Scripture at every point. Should a counselee ask, for instance, "Why do you assign homework? Why is it so necessary when I have gained such ground during the session?" The counselor must have a biblical response ready. In answering this question, he might say something like the following: "Yes, you have moved forward in this session. But that is precisely why homework is necessary. You must now take the next step that is based on that success; you must add works to your faith. James clearly said, 'Faith without works is dead' (James 2:26). Moreover, fruit is supposed to follow repentance. As you make advances in repentance and faith, the assignments are calculated to help you to turn new understandings, new beliefs, and new commitments into fruit and works."

Because of the uniqueness of the purpose of Christian counseling, the counselor will not adopt the methods of non-Christian counselors. "Explain that, if you will," you may say. "Surely, you use talk, listening, and so on, as other counselors do – don't you?" Of course we do. But, you see, talk, listening, and other such elements common to all counseling (and indeed, to all communication) are not methods. They are means. Methods, in contrast, are means committed to the ends of a system. Ventilation, for instance, is a kind of talk that is designed to produce the results that Freud thought would solve his counselees' problems. Non-directive, reflective talk is a method used by Rogerians that is designed to accomplish the goal of drawing people's own ideas out. Rogerians would not use talk to give advice. As you can see, there is talk and there is talk.

Because those who developed each system described problems according to their presuppositions, they set goals that were intended to solve the problems in accordance with those prepositions. They then developed methods that were aimed at moving from the problem to the solution as follows:

Problem → Method → Solution

When descriptions of problems and solutions differ from system to system, methods must differ as well. Since sanctification is the Christian's goal (solution), the methods used by Christian counselors must lead to sanctification. Pagan methods are not designed for that purpose and will not achieve it. Those methods, therefore, must not be employed in Christian counseling. And along with the methods used by Christian counselors…

❖ *The Incentives Are Unique.* Christian counselors should not enter counseling full of fear or uncertainty. Rather, they should begin with great confidence. This confidence does not rest on their own wisdom or ability (though they ought to become as wise and discerning and able to use the Bible as is possible). It depends on the teachings and promises of God. A Christian counselor knows things that the non-Christian does not. He knows that the person who is in trouble is, in one way or another, involved in sin – either his own or another's. Sin is a quantity that other counselors are unfamiliar with and do not deal with. Yet it is the factor behind every problem that ever existed. Already the Christian counselor has an advantage; he understands man's basic problem.[57]

In addition to the fact that Christians have an inerrant source of knowledge about human beings from the Scriptures, they can also promise specific change in response to specific attitudes, commitments, and actions. Whatever God promises in the Bible, the counselor also may promise. He may say, for instance, "If you genuinely repent of the sin of homosexuality, you can live free from it. I tell you this on the basis of I Corinthians 6:9–11, where God's Word says that God enables people to do so."

Moreover, he knows that, in addition to the promise in II Peter 1:3 that he may find in Scripture "everything necessary for life and

---

57 Sin is the broadest category since every problem – even organically based ones – find their cause in Adam's disobedience. Moreover, in the sins of each individual, and those that are committed against him, are included every sort of problem that is imaginable. Non-Christian counselors, and even many eclectic Christians, do not understand this. To focus on one of the problems occasioned by sin (the environment, training, organic difficulties, etc.) rather than on sin itself is a mistake.

godliness," the counselee has dwelling within him the Holy Spirit, Who fights against sin and helps him desire and do those things that please God (cf. Philippians 2:13). This unique combination of the Word and the Spirit acting through the ministry of counseling to produce sanctification means that…

❖ *The Results Are Unique.* The two fundamental results of freeing the stream of sanctification from obstructing logjams are the honor of God and the blessing of His own. These two results can be found nowhere else other than in biblical counseling. If nouthetic counseling is truly unique, why is it that some blunt its uniqueness by attempting to integrate it with other forms of counseling? Precisely because they do not believe that it is unique. It is the fact of the uniqueness of Christian counseling, then, that makes all the difference. This idea will gain acceptance only if its unique character is clearly related to its inseparable attachment to sanctification.

Chapter Eleven

Discipleship

Sanctification is a *daily* matter. We have seen that it is progressive rather than static. All those views that hold to some sort of instantaneous rise to a higher plane of living, either by one act or a series of steps, contradict the words of Jesus who declared that we must *take up the cross daily*. Were we to "arrive" in any sense at some point while we live in this life, Jesus' call would no longer be a daily necessity. Upon "arrival," the call would be dispensed with. Let's look at the exact wording of His call to discipleship:

> Then He said to all of them, "If anybody wants to come after Me, he must deny himself and *take up his cross daily* and follow me" (Luke 9:23, emphasis mine).

First, we must come to an understanding of these words; only then can we look at their implications for sanctification and counseling. Understanding is important because this powerful verse is often misunderstood.

When Jesus used the words "come after me," He was issuing a call to discipleship. The call was different from what we do today when accepting someone into a school. We are too often interested only in academics. The catalogs spell out the content of courses. But it is notable that Jesus did not say merely "sit at My feet." A disciple is, literally, "a student, a pupil," but the idea that a student might merely learn facts that he could recite back to his teacher or replicate on a test was foreign to Hebrew education. One not only learned facts, he learned how to put them into practice (cf. the phrase in Matthew 28:20: "teaching them to *observe*" [emphasis mine]). And, note the important word of our Lord concerning discipling:

> A disciple isn't above his teacher; but everybody who has been thoroughly trained will be like his teacher (Luke 6:40).

Here, He makes the very important statement that effective discipling (thorough "training"), in the end, turns out students who not only *think* like their teacher, but also *become* like him. That was the goal that Jesus had in mind when He invited others to follow Him.[58] They would walk "with Him"[59] and observe what He did as well as learn from His lips what He taught. The whole Person was teaching whole persons.

The reintroduction of discipling into the teaching models of our Christian schools is a very crucial matter, but one that we cannot go into here.[60] For the moment we shall simply note that scholarship, biblically speaking, is a matter of *whole person learning*. It would, therefore, have everything to do with counseling for purposes of sanctification. Sanctification, as we have seen, is concerned with changing one's ways as well as his thoughts.

The second element we examine in the call to discipleship is the phrase "deny himself." The sacerdotalists take this to mean that one is to deny himself something (usually during Lent). That is precisely what Jesus was not saying. Leave out the word

---

58 And others, at length, recognized that the training was effective: "Now when they saw the boldness of Peter and John and realized that they were uneducated laymen, they were surprised and recognized that they had been with Jesus" (Acts 4:13).
59 See also Mark 3:14: "He appointed twelve that they might be with Him and that he might send them out to preach" [emphasis mine].
60 For more on this, see my book *Back to the Blackboard*.

"something" and you will better understand Jesus' words. What He was saying is that one must deny him*self.* But what does it mean to deny one's self? Literally, in Greek the word *deny* means "say 'no.'" To deny self, then, is to say "no" to the desires of self that are out of accord with Christ's will. It is to reject one's own ways of thinking and doing (remember Isaiah 55:8, 9).[61]

Then there are the words "and follow me." That phrase sets forth the alternative to following one's self. The disciple is one who will follow the desires, the thinking, and the walk of the Lord Jesus Christ. He is to say "no" to self, but "yes" to Christ.

Now comes the phrase "and take up his cross." That phrase also has been misconstrued by making it say, "I must take up some burden – an infirmity, the heartaches of a wayward child or a troublesome mother-in-law!" The cross was an instrument of *death*,[62] not merely a burden, and certainly not a lovely gold ornament to hang around the neck. To "take it up" was to carry it to the place where the burden-bearer would be crucified on it (remember the story about Jesus carrying His cross). So to take up one's cross meant to put one's self to death. Crucifixion was a sign of shame and ignominy. He is to die to the desires of his old self. In Colossians 3:5 Paul, possibly referring to Jesus' words, wrote: "So then, put to death the habits of the members of your earthly body." The expression "take up your cross" must not be toned down; it is powerful!

And, finally, we come to the word "daily." This emphasis on a day-by-day crucifixion and denial clearly sets forth the progressive nature of sanctification as over against the instantaneous view. The

---

61 Certainly not those that accord with the Scriptures. See also Proverbs 3:5–7.
62 And not only death, but the death reserved for the worst sort of criminal. See also Philippians 2:6–8.

latter is false because of what Jesus describes as a daily effort[63] to put down sin in one's life and replace it with Jesus' wishes. The difference is vital.

Jesus knew that we would have difficulty following Him; that the sinful thoughts and ways that remain in the believer must be confronted regularly – indeed, on a daily basis. That does not mean that there will be no real victories and that, like AA participants, one must say to himself every day, "I am a drunk." No, according to I Corinthians 6:9 through 11, after listing a number of sins (including drunkenness), Paul says, "Such were some of you." Notice the past tense. That is a very encouraging fact to realize. He raises an expectation that by following the call, one's lifestyle will change. The Believer can put sins behind him. He *can* learn new ways that please God. The disciple is not stuck with his sin. Take, for example, Peter's words:

> ...knowing that you weren't set free from the useless behavior patterns that were passed down from your forefathers, by the payment of a corruptible ransom like silver or gold, but with Christ's valuable blood, shed like the blood of a spotless and unblemished lamb (I Peter 1:18, 19).

Well, what does the emphasis upon "daily" denial and crucifixion mean then? Simply this: throughout this life, there will always be some sin remaining. Regardless of the amount of progress he may make, he will never eradicate all sin. Every day the believer will find that there is a struggle with sin, to which (as Jesus knew) we must die daily. There will always be ideas popping up that are wrong because they are not those of the One Whose faithful disciples we seek to become. He must hear Jesus' clear call and say "no" to the wrong ideas. And because all sin must be replaced with its biblical alternative, we must say "yes" to His ideas

---

[63] Notice the call involves a command, not some passive, quietistic "yielding."

instead. The same must be true of the contrast between our sinful ways and His righteous ones. We must "just say no" – and mean it!

That the believer will make progress by faithful discipleship is inevitable, since it is the method by which one puts off the old lifestyle and puts on the new one. But it will only happen if he develops the discipling attitude that declares, "Today I will say 'no' to sin and 'yes' to righteousness." That sort of phrase might be printed as a motto on counseling materials and handouts.

Now, the Christian counselor who is bent on bringing about sanctification through his counsel will always stress the discipleship dynamic (which is the same as the put off/ put on dynamic)[64]. That is one reason it is virtually impossible to do counseling in one session, as some think. Usually, because many people today are undisciplined, the counselor must "ride herd" on his counselees over a period of time, checking up weekly on their progress. Ordinarily, it takes about six weeks of regular, consistent effort (40 days and 40 nights) to replace a habit. The habit of following the disciple's *daily* duty to say "no" to sin and "yes" to righteousness will develop only in time. To have to report on how well he is following this word from the Lord is helpful in establishing the new dynamic.

Moreover, throughout the weeks of counseling, the counselee's report on his progress in following Christ will help to define the exact nature of his problems and whether or not what is happening in counseling will solve those problems. If, for instance, a counselee is struggling with lust, how well he is succeeding at concentrating on his work rather than lusting after the woman who works next to him at the office should emerge. How well another counselee is doing at holding her tongue when speaking to her husband will also appear. And as one learns to follow the Lord's call, he will see the progress for himself.[65]

---

64 See *The Christian Counselor's Manual* for details.
65 Or the lack of it. There may be, as we said, logjams impeding progress.

Indeed, the counseling of daily denial and following will help the counselor to discover exactly where his counselee is failing. If there is change in what he is or isn't doing, it may be corrected before it is too late and it becomes a habitual error. And if the counselee is simply lapsing in his responsibility to follow Christ, it is then possible to encourage him to heed Jesus' call once more.

An entire series of counseling sessions might easily be conducted in terms of the call to discipleship, which we have seen is a call to sanctification. In each session, this question (or a similar one) may be considered: "Has sanctification been taking place this week? Let's examine it to see what you have been doing or not doing." Then whatever is found, after being examined in the light of actual progress in sanctification, may be looked at from the perspective of what has or has not aided sanctification. If what is found neither leads to nor actually accomplishes sanctification, then measures may be taken to adapt the next week's homework to the situation.

The importance of discipleship-counseling as a way of evaluating progress cannot be over-emphasized. The reason this method of evaluating progress is so appropriate to counseling is that both focus on progress in sanctification. Jesus' discipling methodology of denial-and-following is but one way of saying what Paul and the other apostles described in their letters. The whole Bible teaches a regular, progressive work to be pursued by every disciple.

Chapter Twelve

Grow by Grace

The title of this book and the quotation from II Peter 3:18 on the title page set forth the theme of sanctification that I have been pursuing. In this chapter, I want to take the time to investigate Peter's words. Let me once more quote that verse, this time with the retranslation of but one word – grace:

> But grow by help and the knowledge of our Lord and Savior Jesus Christ.

This command follows a warning to "be on guard" not to be "led astray by the error of lawless persons" lest one lose his "own stability" (v. 17). The instability of untaught persons who "twist" the Scriptures (v. 16), Peter observes, is a major cause of instability in others. The way in which he puts it suggests that such Scripture twisting may be highly contagious. Untaught believers do not understand biblical truth and so lack stability; they may also cause others to lose their own stability. That, according to Peter, is why it is necessary to "grow by grace."

Of course, there are other reasons for growing by grace; some reasons – like the desire to please God – are even more fundamental than the one Peter raises. Nevertheless, this well-known exhortation to grow spiritually, presents one very important motive for growing and another exhortation for biblical counselors to heed. It is not a small matter when false teachers and false teaching twist God's

Word, hindering spiritual growth by knocking the supports out from under counselees so that they too become unstable. Peter says that when the Scriptures are misinterpreted to mean what they were never intended to mean, they can be construed in a way that makes people question various aspects of the faith. And in some cases, the faith itself! When counselors fail to warn counselees, as Peter did – when they fail to expose and counter the false teaching (and sometimes confront those who teach it) as he did in his letters – they betray the Lord and fail to help their counselees as they should. This matter that we are about to consider, then, is important because false teaching may hinder sanctifying growth.

But first, two matters of interpretation: I noted that I had changed one word in the *Christian Counselor's New Testament*, from which I just quoted: it is the word "grace." In the *CCNT*, I translated it "help." Because the word grace is so common, I retained it in the title of the book and when I first quoted this verse. The word "grace" has several meanings, including "unmerited favor" (the best known) and "help" (which is not so well known). In passages where the word applies to believers, it usually means "help," as it does here in II Peter 3:18. Peter is saying that we need the help and the knowledge that the Lord Jesus Christ gives to us. He is the Source of both. Indeed, the "and" in the verse is thought by some to be epexegetical,[66] yielding a rendering something like this: "Help, *even* [i.e., namely] the knowledge of [that comes from] our Lord and Savior, Jesus Christ." Whether or not that is the case, it is obvious that the one sort of help that is mentioned is "knowledge."

There is a second change that I have made in that sentence: I translate the Greek word *en* as "by" instead of "in." It hardly makes sense to speak of growing *in* grace. This becomes especially clear when you recognize that Peter is talking about "help." How would

---

[66] This means that the second element (knowledge) further explains the first (help). The kind of help in view is the provision of knowledge that one needs to confront error.

you possibly grow *in* help? In its instrumental use,[67] *en* may be rightly translated "by." The important thing here is this – Jesus gives His people knowledge that enables them to grow strong enough to withstand the false teaching that might otherwise lead them astray. He is relating sanctification, as it produces stability, to knowledge.

The counselor, as a result, must become a teacher of biblical knowledge. True counselors always bring knowledge to the counseling session. That is why a counselor must be a "knowledgeable" person who "rightly handles the Word of truth" (II Timothy 2:15). After all, he is to be concerned about his counselee; that is a given. But he is also to be concerned about those who are unstable and untaught. As Paul taught, "in meekness" he must correct "those who oppose [God's truth], in hope that God may bring them by repentance into the full knowledge of the truth" (II Timothy 2:25). Growth, then, comes through "knowledge." It is questionable whether growth ever occurs apart from it.

Think about that last statement of Peter's for a bit. Peter contrasts untaught instability with certain knowledge. A person simply cannot grow as he should if he is unstable. For example, if someone who has for a time understood the biblical teaching of the perseverance of the saints, subsequently is seduced into questioning that doctrine because of the teaching of someone who does not have a clear knowledge of biblical teaching, it will adversely affect his growth. This flawed teaching may cause him to focus on himself rather than on pleasing God and showing love for others. The sanctification process will be seriously hindered. Indeed, uncertainty of salvation could cause a logjam that might easily set back his spiritual growth significantly.

---

67 To think of this as a spherical dative, inferring that one grows in the sphere of grace, is much more difficult. Either way, Peter speaks of the *help* one receives from Christ, emphasizing how that help involves *knowledge*. Knowledge, of course, is what those who have fallen victim to the twisted teaching of untaught, unstable persons need.

Paul spoke about the importance of becoming rooted firmly in the Bible so as to become mature in the faith. Here is what he said in Ephesians 4:13 and 14:

> …until we all attain to the unity of the faith and to the full knowledge of God's Son, to mature manhood, to the point where we become as fully adult as Christ. This must happen so that we may no longer be infants, blown about and carried around by every wind of teaching, by human trickery, by craftiness designed to lead to error.

Notice in both passages, the apostles stress the importance of knowledge as the antidote to false teaching.

Now, it is also worthwhile noting that Peter says those who come to deceive will come with the Scriptures. They like to assert the authority of the Scriptures to bolster their errors, but they twist them in order to make them fit their beliefs and teachings. There are too many counselees who will accept as true anything a teacher says so long as he mentions the Scriptures. But here, Peter warns that not everyone who uses the Scriptures may be trusted. Many twist them. So it is not enough for someone to represent himself as a *Bible* teacher. How does he handle the Bible? Is his teaching that of someone who is "untaught" in the Word? There are many who, with very little understanding of what Scripture means, take it upon themselves to teach others. Just because one has the money to buy radio or TV time does not mean he is knowledgeable in the things concerning the faith. Counselees must be taught to examine all new teachings carefully. They should compare them with the historic confessions of the church and ask for their pastor's opinion before accepting them. Because many did not do this, the "untaught" William Miller (who himself was a believer) spawned two Adventist cults![68]

---

[68] The Adventists (eventually becoming the Seventh Day Adventists) and, through them, the Jehovah's Witnesses.

So growth comes by the help that Jesus gives. We have already mentioned that Jesus sent the Holy Spirit to dwell within us to enable us to understand His Word. And one purpose of that understanding is to be able to avoid being deceived by false teaching. John wrote:

> Let that which you have heard from the beginning remain in you… I wrote these things to you about those who are misleading you. But the Anointing that you have received from Him [the Holy Spirit] remains in you and you don't need anybody to teach you. Rather, since His Anointing teaches you about everything (and is true, and doesn't lie), remain in Him even as He has taught you (I John 2:24, 26, 27).

Clearly, one function of the Spirit with whom we were anointed at baptism (cf. I Corinthians 12:13) is to enable us to comprehend and apply what the apostles taught. God's concern is for us to obtain knowledge of Him and His will because knowledge is so closely associated with growth. That knowledge is not extra-biblical but biblical. So then, growth comes from the Spirit, enabling us to become knowledgeable about biblical teaching by helping us to interpret and apply His Word correctly. That is the bottom line.

Every counselor, then, ought to warn about the unstable teachings of untaught persons – who abound in our society. And they must teach counselees the basic truths from Scripture that apply to their situations. Moreover, they would do well to urge every counselee to take a course in Bible interpretation. After all, to send a counselee who has been "led astray" back where people may lead him astray again, unprepared, without warning and buttressing him against such errors as much as possible, is simply poor counseling.

The trouble is that there are too many counselors who are afraid to tackle doctrine – even when it is a large part of a counselee's problem.[69] Not only is that poor counseling, it is usually cowardly. Or, in other cases, the counselor may not know enough doctrine himself to handle the aberrant teachings that his counselee has imbibed. If either of these is true of you, shame on you, counselor! Don't wait another day before hitting the books to discover what you need to know to help that counselee. And study the Scriptures so regularly that the next time there is such a problem, you will be prepared to meet it.[70]

So, knowledge brings about growth. It "helps" in many ways. And the help and knowledge that Jesus gives your counselees to assist them to grow in sanctification may very likely be by means of you!

---

69 The writers of the New Testament, and Jesus Himself, are not hesitant to refute false doctrine. It is a mistake to think that such refutation can be avoided. While one must refute in meekness, as we have seen, nevertheless, he must do it! The Bible has much to say about this matter.

70 Too many counselors study books about counseling (like this one) rather than the Bible and those books that will help them properly interpret it without twisting it. Unfortunately, it is in books about counseling that one often finds some of the poorest interpretations of the Scriptures!

Chapter Thirteen

How Much Growth Is Possible?

In contrast to the perfectionists and the victorious life people, there have been those throughout the history of the church who have taught that very little Christian growth is possible. Their overemphasis on sin in the regenerate almost cancels out the presence and power of the Holy Spirit, Who is at work in a regenerate person's life sanctifying him. Both of these extreme emphases are unscriptural.

Surely the Spirit, with His sovereign power, is capable of overcoming any sin He wishes. And since He took up residence in Christians to do that work, there should be every expectation that He will be doing it (cf. Philippians 1:6). Surely, as Paul said, God produces in us "both the willingness and the ability to do the things that please Him" (Philippians 2:13). Surely His power enables believers to put behind them many sinful lifestyles (see I Corinthians 6:9-11). Keeping these facts in mind, then, let us explore something of the possibilities for achieving sanctifying growth in counselees.

It is important for the counselor to be clear about the possibilities for achieving growth. Low expectations or ultra-high ones will have a lot to do with how he counsels. Interestingly enough, both of these extremes end up causing the same result: the counselor makes too little effort to bring about change. On the one hand, if little can be expected, the counselor will aim too low and settle for less than he ought. On the other hand, if the counselor thinks that in some instantaneous manner his counselee will be wafted up to heights of victory, obviously there will be little for him to do. Both views tend to limit the amount of counseling activity.

The biblical counselor, however, recognizes that true growth in living for Christ may require much counseling. The counselor and the believer, in cooperation with the Spirit and prayerfully using the Word, must struggle for growth and fight against all the internal and external forces that would inhibit it.

The very image of growth indicates that sanctification takes time, takes cultivation, and takes care. Healthy plants that produce "much fruit" also require pruning by the Word (cf. John 15:1–5).[71] The phrase "much fruit" is important to the discussion that we have undertaken in this chapter. The Lord Jesus not only postulates its possibility but *expects* the believer to produce "much fruit"; when he does not, counseling may be called for. Jesus holds out the prospect of *much* fruit – not very little but also not a hundred percent yield.

In His comments on fruit-bearing, the Lord also told us what it would take for successful fruit-growing. He told the disciples that He had "pruned" them by His "word" (John 15:3). There can be little doubt that the same is true today as well. Once again we see that it is the Word of God – today found only in the Scriptures of the Old and the New Testaments – that brings about sanctification. Therefore, counselors must become aware of the utter importance of the Word for sanctification in counseling.

Of course, the prerequisite to all fruit-bearing is remaining in Christ, Who declared: "Just as the branch can't bear fruit on its

---

71 In many ways, the counselor may view himself as a vinedresser whose task is to prune the "plants" that God sends his way so that they may bear much fruit. To do this, he must know how to deftly wield the sharp knife of Scripture in a responsible manner.

own (unless it stays on the vine), so you can't unless you stay in Me" (John 15:4). *Staying* or *remaining* (in the KJV, "abiding") in the vine has to do not with some quietistic "resting" but, rather, with perseverance: "unless a person stays in Me, he is thrown outside like a branch and withers; they gather them, throw them into the fire and burn them" (John 15:6). Clearly, it is not true believers who are discarded and burned, but those who make a false profession of faith. How can they be known? They do not persevere.

But to those who remain until the end, Jesus gives assurance that they will bear much fruit. Not only does He assure us that this is true, He also indicates that it is normal to anticipate this sort of abundance. I cannot stress strongly enough, then, that the believer should settle for nothing less than that which the Lord holds forth – "much fruit."

Again, the manner of growing is to "cleanse" oneself from both inner and outer corruption, as Paul wrote in II Corinthians 7:1, "Since we have these promises, dear friends, we must cleanse ourselves from every pollution of flesh and spirit, completing our holiness out of fear for God." To cleanse from pollution is but another term for pruning (literally, "cleansing") sinful practices. But once more note the "promises" of the Scriptures (quoted in II Corinthians 6:16–18) are the basis for the cleansing process. In the passage quoted from the Old Testament, God commands them to "come out from their midst and be separate." The call to "*be separate*" is a call to sanctification. Stressing biblical calls to sanctification are of importance in helping counselees to grow. The biblical call must be echoed by the counselor, heard by the counselee, enforced by the Spirit, and performed by His help. When that happens, blossoms will appear, grow, bud, and produce much fruit.

The end of the matter is this: "My Father is glorified by this – that you bear much fruit; then you will be My disciples" (John 15:8). In other words, to be a true disciple is to bear much fruit. If a person does not produce fruit, then we must question his salvation. After all, the goal of the Christian's life ought to be to glorify God. If in some sense he does not bring glory to God, he is not fulfilling his purpose as a disciple. Jesus says fruit in the Christian's life is what spreads God's fame among others. This point agrees with His words in Matthew 7:20: "So it is from their fruit that you will know them." Indeed, all of this is but a further exposition of Jesus' command, "Let your light shine in the presence of people so that they may see your fine deeds and glorify your Father Who is in the heavens" (Matthew 5:16).

There is no question about how much growth is possible – much! That is Christ's word.

Chapter Fourteen

Does Suffering Sanctify?

It depends. The Bible certainly gives every indication that God uses trials and suffering to help His children grow – but only when they handle it correctly. At the beginning of his letter, James urges his readers, "My brothers, consider it a happy situation when you fall into trials of various sorts" (James 1:2). How can he say that? He goes on, "knowing that the testing of your faith works endurance" (v. 3). So, James explains, testings of all sorts can help a Christian learn how to endure. But then he continues, "Let endurance have its full effect, that you may be complete and entire, lacking nothing" (v. 4). There seems to be in these words a warning that one may curtail the sanctifying process in such a way that its full effect may not be enjoyed. The completion of the process may be cut short. Sanctification through suffering doesn't take place automatically.

This is what so often happens when Christians are in a privileged position to grow: in one way or another, they step in and stop their own growth. What usually happens, as James goes on to say, is that we fail to ask for the "wisdom" that we ought to derive from the experience (v. 5). And when we do ask, we often ask with weak faith, full of doubts about how the trial we are undergoing could possibly be for our sanctification (v. 6).

In such cases, we will receive nothing from the Lord by way of understanding (v. 7) because "a double-minded person is unstable in all his ways" (v. 8). God graciously answers the prayer of faith without reproaching us for our lack of wisdom and grants the wisdom when it is needed to undergo the trial and to grow in grace. It is plain, then, that trials may be a blessing, not in and of themselves (the Christian is not a masochist), but in the results they may produce. Trials can be an integral part of our sanctification.

"But if there were no trials, there would be no need for endurance." I can hear this objection. Yes, this is true, but we live in a world of sin, and sin brings about "trials of various sorts." The smaller ones teach us how to endure so that when the larger ones appear, we know what to do. We will have learned how to endure. In other words, the trials that come may be turned into valuable resources for growth in handling future trials. But to doubt their efficacy is to cut off the benefits. Instead, what we ought to do is ask for wisdom to see how we can profit from each trial.

Here, counselors can be of great benefit in helping counselees to get the most blessing from the various trials they must go through. Very few counselees understand what James said. They must be instructed and helped to see that trials, when handled God's way, are a means of grace – a way in which God makes us more like Christ. Jesus also endured trials and was the better for them.[72] So can we become better through suffering. He learned obedience by means of suffering and achieved salvation for us! Note that more than one benefit may be derived from trials and suffering. Both He and we benefited from His suffering. If even Jesus, as man, had to learn from suffering, then surely we must as well.

---

72 "Even though He was a Son, He learned obedience from what he suffered; and having been perfected, He became the Origin of eternal salvation to those who obey Him" (Hebrews 5:8, 9).

Through the ages, the people of God have learned how to grow by means of the grace (help) of suffering (i.e., that suffering provides). Listen to these words from Psalm 119:

> Before I was afflicted I went astray, but now I have kept Your Word (v. 67, NKJV).

> It is good that I was afflicted that I might learn Your statutes (v. 71, NKJV).

> Yahweh, I know that Your judgments are righteous, and that it is in faithfulness that You have afflicted me (v. 75).

> Unless Your law had been my delight, long ago I would have perished in my affliction (v. 92).

> Affliction and pressure have seized me, but Your commandments are my delight (v. 143).

In all of these verses, we see one thing: the Word of God helped the Psalmist to turn affliction into profit. The counselor will be remiss if he does not encourage his counselee when suffering to find the direction, the sustenance he needs, the answers, and the encouragement to handle trials that are found in the Bible.

In Psalm 119:92, it is clear from his words that the psalmist could not have endured the suffering he was experiencing apart from the Scriptures in which he delighted. That "delight," presumably, came from familiarity with the law of God before the suffering so that when it appeared, he was able to turn to those truths to sustain him. Otherwise, he might have succumbed to the trial.

Not everyone must know the Bible thoroughly before undergoing trial, however. At an earlier point in his life, the psalmist learned how beneficial the Scriptures are *by undergoing suffering* (v. 71). In verse 67, he makes the point that before his affliction, he wandered out of God's pathways, but his affliction brought him back to the Scriptures to find his way. The trial itself drove him to God's Word so that he might once more learn to walk in His ways.

How was it that the Bible (God's "judgments") instructed and comforted him in trial? He says in verse 75 that from them he learned that all affliction that God sent his way was for his good: "In faithfulness You have afflicted me." God was not bringing something unjust into his life; from His perspective (regardless of what other people meant to do to him)[73] the intention was a faithful one. God had not forsaken him. Actually, He was working out something good for him.

Paul also noted how his suffering was given for his sanctification in order to keep him from becoming proud. He had been caught up into the third heaven, had seen wonderful things, and was given a "thorn in the flesh" to keep him from boasting (II Corinthians 12:2). This physical affliction (a seriously impairing eye condition, perhaps) helped keep him humble. So even extreme difficulties may be intended by God for a blessing. After praying three times that God would remove the condition, at last he came to see that it was designed by God as a blessing, and he could write about it that way. That passage is one that many counselees have found to be of comfort when they were suffering from some physical illness or affliction. Countering pride may not always be the benefit derived, but some benefit may always be found in sickness if one is on the alert to find it.

---

73 See also Genesis 50:20. Joseph's brothers planned to do evil to him, but God planned to do good through their evil act and to save the people of Israel, from whom the Messiah would come, from perishing during the famine. Once again, the double intention – man's and God's – is made clear. Counselors must help counselees to turn from what men intend (which is where their focus so often lies) to what the Bible says God, in faithfulness, is doing for them. Even when they cannot see the outcome until much later, as in Joseph's case, they can be taught the truth of Romans 8:28, 29.

So we see that everything depends upon how a trial or affliction is handled. And the way in which one comes to correctly evaluate the trial is by applying the teachings of the Bible to the situation. But the wicked – and even God's people at times – fail to do so. Rather, they may turn farther away from God, or against Him, as the result of trials. Take the case of Pharaoh. Here was a man who had several opportunities to repent and humble himself before God. But instead, he hardened his heart!

Look at God's people. Jeremiah wrote,

> O Lord, do not Thy eyes search for truth? Thou hast beaten them, but they felt no rebuke; Thou hast disciplined them, but they spurned correction. They have made their faces harder than flint; they have refused to repent (Jeremiah 5:3, Berkeley).

That is exactly the wrong response to suffering. Here were people who named the Name of the Lord *wasting* their suffering. That is the best you can say for them. They failed to profit from it. God sent affliction to bring them to repentance and, instead of repenting, they became hardened. Some counselees will be exactly like that. No matter how you show them God's will from the Scriptures, no matter how severely God punishes them for their sin, their response is the opposite of what it should be. The passage in Jeremiah would be a good one to read to such persons as a warning, hoping that they would stop wasting their suffering.

Contrast the Apostle Paul, who often spoke of his sufferings for Christ. Here was a man mightily used of God – partly because he seemed always to benefit from suffering. Listen to these words:

> We are afflicted in all sorts of ways, but not crushed; perplexed, but not given to despair; persecuted, but not deserted; struck down, but not destroyed.... Now all of this is for your sake so that as grace spreads to more and more people it may result in an overflowing

of thanksgiving to God's glory (II Corinthians 4:8– 9, 15).

It is clear that Paul looked away from the present suffering to the result coming from it. In one way or another he saw that his suffering would bless people and glorify God. How important it is for counselees to be taught to do the same!

Paul continues,

> As a result, we don't give up, even though our outer person is decaying, because our inner person is being renewed daily. This temporary light affliction is producing for us an eternal weight of glory that is beyond all comparison, since we aren't looking for the things that are seen, but rather for the things that are unseen. The things that are seen are temporary, but the things that are unseen are eternal (II Corinthians 4:16–18)

It is utterly amazing that Paul could call his suffering "light affliction"! All one need do is to read the lists of sufferings in chapters 6:4–10 and 11:22–29 in this very book of II Corinthians to see how extensive they were. I suggest that you do so for counselees to show what it was that he could call "light afflictions." How could he do it?

He explains by citing two facts: first, he was receiving daily inward renewal from God. Certainly, he was sustained by prayer and the reading of the Word. Second, he kept his eye fixed on eternity. He saw the reward as did the suffering saints of old (Hebrews 11:13–16). Jesus encouraged us to do this in Matthew 6:19-21, when He urged us to store up treasures in heaven, and He explained, "Where your treasure is, there is where your heart will be too" (v. 21). Here is the ultimate key to enduring and to benefiting from suffering. Sanctification is achieved as one fixes his heart on the things that are eternal. That is what makes him of earthly good now!

Counselor, do you often talk to your counselees about the *results* of affliction? Do you help them to fix their eyes on eternity? Do you urge them not to lose the blessings of suffering? Do you point them to how sufferings may enable them to grow? You should.

Chapter Fifteen
Sanctification and Obedience

Obedience is intimately connected to counseling and to sanctification. In giving the great commission, the Lord Jesus commanded,

> Go, therefore, and disciple all nations, baptizing them into the Name of the Father and of the Son and of the Holy Spirit, teaching them to observe all that I have commanded you (Matthew 28:19, 20).

Here is a command to teach disciples to observe all of Christ's commands. The command to disciple those in "all nations" is in educational terms. It included the task of teaching. But the kind of education that is in view is a Hebrew form of education, not ours. This teaching requires not the mere imparting of facts, but the discipling of those who are taught. It is education that brings about change in the lifestyle of the disciple (student).[74] But notice that the education is pictured by Jesus as teaching that leads to the "observance of His commands." What do these words mean?

First of all, note that this command to disciple and teach comes in a certain context. The word "therefore,"[75] which begins this sentence, refers back to verse 18 in which Jesus declared to

---
74 See the earlier discussion of this matter in Chapter Eleven. For the greatest detail, see my book *Teaching to Observe*.
75 Greek, *oun*.

the eleven disciples: "All authority in heaven and on earth has been given to Me." Here, proleptically,[76] Jesus declares that all the sovereign authority (Greek, *exousia*) of God had been granted to Him as the God-man over everything and everyone in the heavens and on the earth.

He is making it clear that as they went[77] preaching the gospel they would be received by all the *Gentiles* (perhaps the better translation of *ethne* here,[78] since that was the unique thing about their mission: the gospel was to go into all the world to all the Gentiles rather than to Jews alone). This reception would lead to discipleship as those who believed were baptized into (became a part of) the church that bears the Name of the Trinity.

Once having matriculated into the school of Christ through baptism (the admitting ordinance into the visible church, which here is pictured as a school), His disciples (pupils, students) were to be *taught*. After all, that is what a school is all about. And what they were to be taught was the commandments of Christ. Now, commandments are given not merely for knowledge; they are handed down to be obeyed by those who receive them. To speak of "observing" (Greek, *terein*) commandments is but another way of saying *obeying* them. Thus the life of the believer is pictured as a life of discipling, in which he is learning to obey Christ's commands to him. It is, therefore, a life of sanctification.

---

76 That is, speaking of something that is just about to happen as if it already had happened. At Jesus' ascension He would be "crowned with glory and honor" (Hebrews 2:9).
77 Literally, "as you go"; there is no command to go. It is assumed that they would.
78 The word *ethne* may be rightly translated either "nations" or "Gentiles." Both are equally possible. The New Testament period was one in which the church would consist of converted Jews and Gentiles alike. So already in his day John could speak of those "persons" that Christ "bought for God from every tribe and tongue and people and nation" (Revelation 5:9; see also Revelation 7:9; 20:2, 3).

Sanctification and Obedience

In a similar way, Paul speaks of conversion as a change of masters from sin to God: "But thank God that you, who were once slaves of sin, now have obeyed from the heart the pattern of teaching to which you were handed over" (Romans 6:17). And he goes on to explain:

> In the same way that you presented your members as slaves to uncleanness and lawlessness to bring about more lawlessness, now you must present your members as slaves of righteousness to bring about sanctification (Romans 6:19).

Notice how "sanctification" is the new goal of God's redeemed servant over against "lawlessness," which was his goal when he was still the slave of sin. Obeying Christ's law from the heart is the same as keeping (observing, obeying) His commandments. So it is quite clear that discipleship, which at its heart consists of learning to obey Christ, is the means of reaching the goal of such teaching – sanctification.[79] There can be no question about the centrality of obedience in discipleship or about its result – sanctification. Calvin understood this centrality and featured it when he wrote, "nothing is more acceptable to him [God] than obedience."[80]

Obedience is always to commands. It is not abstract. There are those who think that there are no commands to be obeyed today but the command to love. That is quite wrong. Not only does Jesus speak of "all things" (everything) that He commanded during His earthly ministry, but also in the books of the New Testament the obvious fact is that Jesus had laid down orders about

---

79 See also Romans 6:22, where Paul speaks of the "fruit" (*result*) of the new obedience as "sanctification." Thus one "presents" the members of his body to God for the purpose of working righteousness, which comes by obeying the commandments of Christ ("pattern of teaching") from the heart. And the "fruit" of obedience is sanctification. This sanctification, he says, results in "eternal life."
80 *The Institutes of the Christian Religion*, Book 2, Chapter 8, Section 5.

many things.[81] To obey specific commands, in fact, is the way in which one demonstrates his love. Quietism, of the sort that often opposes counseling which points to the specific commands of the Bible, leaves the counselee up a tree. He simply doesn't know what he must do in order to "love." Love becomes an amorphous thing, perhaps in many cases a mere feeling.

But love in the Scriptures is closely associated with action. It is not passive. "God so loved the world that He *gave…*" (John 3:16; cf. Gal 2:20; Ephesians 5:25). And it is associated with commandments, such as "love your enemies" (Matthew 5:44), which was one of the commandments that Christ gave us to obey. Note that love is *commanded*. It takes place when one *obeys* (clearly, it is more than a feeling). But how is it to be fulfilled? To *show* love to one's enemies, he is to *give* him something to eat or drink if he is hungry or thirsty (Romans 12:20).[82] In John 14:15, Jesus sums all of this up in one pregnant explanation: "If you love Me, keep My commandments." Nothing more on the point need be said!

"But that sounds like legalism," someone may say. One of the most frequently expressed errors is to label the call to obedience to Christ's commands "legalistic." Every counselor will face this false charge from time to time. Actually, there is much talk about

---

81 In I Corinthians 7:25, Paul writes, "Now I don't have any order from the Lord about virgins," implying that He did give orders about other things. And, through the Spirit, He was now giving orders through the Apostle (v. 40). See also Titus 2:15: "Speak these things; urge and convict, with recognition that you have full authority to give orders. Let nobody disregard you." Clearly, not only in Person, but through the apostles, Jesus Christ gave His people many commands that were to be obeyed. These were given in order to lead to sanctification, as we see. This means that the counselor will set biblical commands before his counselees and expect them to obey them.

82 The principle is to do what you are able to do to meet an enemy's need.

legalism, but very little explanation of it. The term is loosely slung about without precise understanding. One reason for this is that legalism has been often referred to but very seldom discussed at length. There are few discussions of the matter in print (when found, they are usually but a part of some other discussion, as in this chapter). I once searched through two voluminous seminary libraries for books on the subject and found none in one and only one in the other. And in the scattered, brief references to legalism that one does find, legalism is almost always discussed in its relationship to justification not to sanctification.

In terms of legalism's relationship to justification, legalism reeks of a view of salvation by merit.[83] The problem that Paul fought was in relationship to the judaizing of the churches. He was interested not only in the matter of the false teaching of salvation (justification) by works, but also in teaching of sanctification (growing) by works alone. He wrote, for instance:

> Galatians, you are stupid! Who has put a spell on you, you before whose eyes Jesus Christ Jesus Christ was placarded as the crucified One? Tell me this one thing: did you receive the Spirit from works of law, or from hearing with faith? Are you really so stupid? Having begun by the Spirit are you now going to be completed by the flesh? (Galatians 3:1–3)

His concern was to show that the process of sanctification, or being "completed" (Greek, *epiteleo*) by works, was not what Christian living is all about. Later on, in Galatians 5, Paul shows that the characteristics of sanctification (or holiness) that he lists are truly the fruit of the *Spirit*. Legalism, then, is a matter of seeking

---

83 In relationship to justification, counselors must be careful not to counsel unbelievers. To do so is to cause them to think that they please God by moving from one unbiblical lifestyle to another. I have discussed this matter earlier in the book.

to become sanctified by works *apart from the Spirit*. However, it is not wrong to insist on obedience *by means of the Spirit*. In terms of counseling, legalism is not a matter of insisting on obedience to Christ's commands, but of teaching that *mere conformity* to those commands will enable counselees to grow in holiness. It consists of depending on those commandments to change the counselee rather than depending on the Spirit to enable him to change.

So there is a legalism of thought and attitude as well as a legalism of action. The first precedes the second. If an act itself is considered meritorious, the counselee will not only take unfounded pride in what he does (rather than giving the credit to God); but in the end will also fail to observe Christ's commandments. That is because he will not have obeyed "from the heart." To obey from the heart is to obey genuinely; it means that outward conformity alone is unacceptable. Jesus again and again spoke of the inner intent as necessary to the acceptability of the outer action (cf. Matthew 5:27–28). The inner intent of the counselee must correspond to the inner intent of the command. The rich young ruler (Luke 18:18–23) obeyed God's commands outwardly, but loved money more than God or his neighbor. Christ's assignment to sell all he had and give the money he received to the poor and then to follow Him exposed his interior thinking and attitude that was out of sync with his outer conformity. He obeyed, but not "from the heart."

To obey in human wisdom and strength, then, is legalism. But to obey the Word by the Spirit is not. All other forms of counseling are legalistic; biblical counseling alone assumes that the Spirit is necessary for effecting sanctification. He is the "Spirit of holiness" (Romans 1:4) Who works through His Word (John 17:17) to change both actions and intentions. When counselors help counselees to develop new biblical habits to replace old ones, for instance, they encourage them to ask God to change not only externals but also to change their hearts. Peter speaks of "hearts trained in greed" (II Peter 2:14). The heart is where the habit is.

"Heart," in Scripture, includes the brain and the mind. The heart must be changed as the habit is; the habit will be changed as the heart is. The one cannot be divorced from the other. Holiness is first and foremost an inside job! To encourage counselees merely to change their outer behavior is to create hypocritical counselees and to make God out to be nothing more than a *decorative* God Who superficially paints over the rotten wood beneath! The biblical counselor must stress prayer, the work of the Spirit, and the Word in enabling him to obey. God is an Interior Decorator.

Legalism, in connection with counseling, is setting a counselee out on a pathway that is doomed to failure because it sets him out to do what he cannot do alone. He must be aided by the knowledge that comes from the Word and the insight and power that comes from the Spirit. Counselors will take heed to this matter because it is central to pleasing God by properly breaking the logjam that impedes sanctification.

But how does one obey that which he does not want to obey? If he does, isn't that legalism? I have heard people say such things. On the one hand, if he obeys *merely* out of duty, of course, that is wrong. But, on the other hand, he may rightly obey when he loathes doing so. "Really?" you ask. Yes. Think of Christ, Who did not want to go to the cross, Who sweat drops of blood over contemplating becoming viewed as a sinner by His Father. He did so, but not because He wanted to. Similarly, a counselee may be called on to do what he does not want to do (for example, loving an enemy). He may ask, "But how can that be? Isn't that the height of legalism? Pharisaism?"

Not if what he does is done out of love for God! One must have the inner desire to please God when out of duty he obeys a commandment that is not pleasant to obey. A housewife cleans the toilets not because she enjoys the chore but because she loves her family. A counselee may be called on to obey a command out of love for God and his neighbor, even when he does not look forward to the task itself. That is what must be stressed. The counselee must understand that in his inner person, he must not do anything God commands for brownie points; he must obey out of love.

The importance of obedience in its relationship to sanctification through the Spirit is plainly stated by Peter in I Peter 1:2 where Peter says that the Spirit sanctifies so that we may obey. One grows by obedience, but that obedience – properly accomplished through the wisdom and power of the Spirit – is itself the result of previous sanctification. When the Spirit sanctifies in order to enable us to obey, He so changes our desires and abilities that we are able to do those tasks which are undesirable in themselves (cf. Philippians 2:13). So intimately connected are sanctification and obedience then that, once begun, they each produce the other in a chicken-and-egg fashion. The counselor who recognizes this dynamic may break in at either the point of obedience or at the point of thought and intent, so long as he ties both of these together as the Bible does.

Chapter Sixteen
Conclusion

One thing ought to be unmistakable: sanctification is critical to counseling. Indeed, as we have seen, counseling is also critical to sanctification. The two stand or fall together. If you are speaking of truly Christian counseling, you are speaking about counseling that assists the process of sanctification whenever it becomes slowed down, halted, or reversed. In fact, the purpose of biblical counseling is nothing other than to enable the Christian to become more like Christ.

On the other hand, a measure of sanctification in the counselee is required for counseling to succeed. The counselee must repent of sin (itself a step in sanctification) in order to break many logjams. He must then take other sanctification steps in order to move ahead with fruit that will not only give evidence of, but also shore up, repentance. So once begun, the process reinforces itself. That shows how intimately the two are bound up in one another.

There is no doubt that, in order to counsel biblically, a counselor must understand sanctification as it is set forth in the Scriptures. If a would-be counselor has a faulty view of sanctification, he will counsel wrongly. That is why this book is necessary. It is intended both to warn and to instruct. As one who would counsel, if you don't fully understand sanctification, if you have any doubts about any aspect of it, if you are unsure that counseling is deeply involved in the sanctification process, please do not counsel until you have settled all these matters biblically. I cannot say it strongly enough – simply stop, study, and learn!

I have shown that counseling is not important in itself, and if logjams in the process of sanctification did not occur, it would be unnecessary. But they do occur, so counseling is necessary. Proper counseling is dependent on a proper doctrinal understanding of sanctification, once more proving that counseling is doctrinal. Bill Goode, former director of the National Association of Nouthetic Counselors, was absolutely correct when he stated that "all counseling problems are theological problems." I would add that all counseling solutions are theological solutions!

Is
All Truth
God's Truth?

Jay E. Adams

Contents

Introduction 111
Truth is God's Truth 113
Since Truth is God's Truth… 118
Solving the Problems 122
Serious Matters 128
Revelation 134
No Consensus 142
Can You Call This "God's Truth"? 148
Conflicting "Revelations"? 154
Psychological Empiricism 160
So What? 165

Introduction

Recently, the prospective pastor of a new congregation and the core group could not get together because, among other things, the preacher affirmed that "All truth is God's truth." How could that have been a stumbling block? Well, as he went on to explain, he meant psychology has much truth to offer and he intended to use the findings of that "discipline" in his ministry. Members of the core group differed with him and, graciously, the pastor and the group parted company because they found it impossible to work together. Clearly, the sticking point was the declaration that "All truth is God's truth." How can this be? How can Christians differ over such a matter? Isn't all truth God's truth? Is there some other "truth" out there – separate from God and over against *His* truth? Were the members of the core group right in differing with the preacher, or were they wrong?

The declaration which separated the core group from the prospective pastor has become a catchword or *slogan*. It is bandied about, sometimes with little or no understanding of what is implied. Indeed, many times it is used to silence those who do not think that psychological practices should be used in Christian counseling. Merely by stating it, the psychology advocate thinks he has settled the argument. Presumably, the pastor in question did some of those very things.

But once again, can anyone deny that all truth is God's truth? That truth is the possession of God Who is its source?

Is All Truth God's Truth?

Should not the slogan be a truism for *every* Christian? Surely those who differed with the pastor must have had a reason. Were they stubborn obscurantists, ignorant of what they were discussing? Or were they simply untrained laymen who were unable to handle such philosophical matters?

It is these questions and the fallout from their answers that I wish to discuss in this book. Among the many issues that exist in the Church and have vexed sincere Christians, who want to accept all the truth that comes from God, there are few more vexing than this one. While such Christians remain hesitant about the inclusion of psychology in Christian counseling, the affirmation that "All truth is God's truth" seems to make their "no psychology" position untenable. So, in their perplexity, many uneasily go along. Others, who believe that they sense that something about the slogan is very wrong but can't articulate what it is, may simply withdraw from the discussion into their shell, while the "All truth" people triumphantly ride off into the sunset.

Are people like those in the core group bigoted, biased beyond reaching, or hopelessly prejudiced? Must they be shown that they are inconsistent in declaring their belief in God's truth while rejecting that which comes from sources other than the Bible? In this book I shall examine the claim that "All truth is God's truth." Can the slogan, as the pastor used it, stand scrutiny? Does the claim have merit? Is psychology a source of "God's truth"? Or is there a good reason why the group rejected the prospective pastor's explanation of the slogan? You may be surprised at the answer to that question.

Chapter One

Truth *is* God's Truth

Origin of the Slogan

In the nineteen-forties Frank Gabelein, headmaster of the Stony Brook School in New York, was using the slogan. Whether or not he was the first to do so is not easy to determine, but it is possible (as some think) that he was the one who originated it.[1] Regardless, over the intervening years, book after book has included it as if it were the author's astonishing new insight. We must take time to consider the validity of the claim that the slogan makes. Is what it affirms about truth true?

A Good Slogan

In order to answer that question, let's take a look at the slogan itself. There is nothing wrong about it. Indeed, it is a fine expression of the biblical viewpoint. For one thing, it expresses the fact that truth is one. Error is manifold. There are many ways of being wrong; there is only one way of being right. So all truth – that which is "truly"[2] true – since it is true, is definitely "God's truth." That is to say, it stems from Him and exactly corresponds

---

1 His use of the phrase was applied generally, and not specifically to counseling.
2 It is difficult to express the thought without resorting to such a construction.

to His view of things. That which is true conforms to what God knows to be true.

Understanding Truth

But what is truth? Pilate asked the question yet it seems that he never learned the answer. If he had only known that standing before him was the One Who is "the Way, the Truth and the Life" (John 14:6) he might not have been so glib about the matter. Yes, in the final analysis, it is Jesus Christ Who is the Truth. As John wrote, "grace and truth came through Jesus Christ" (John 1:17). He is the One Who made God's truth available to mankind. In Him, not only was the Word of truth spoken, but by His attitudes and actions truth became visible; He, himself, was the Word from God:

> At the beginning, the Word already existed, and the Word was with God and the Word was God … the Word became flesh and tented among us, and we saw His glory, glory like that which a unique son receives from his father, full of grace and truth (John 1:1, 14).

Now, what does that mean? How are we to understand it? Well, a word is the expression of someone's thought. The form of the verb "to be" ("already existed") means that at the "beginning" (origin) of the creation God the Son already existed. He did not derive His knowledge of truth from the creation; rather, as the eternal Word, truth already existed in Him. Indeed, He assisted the Father in creation (John 1:3). Part of His earthly mission was to reveal God's thoughts and ways to men. In other words, to reveal truth. That means the living Word is the Standard of truth and whatever claims to be truth must be measured by what He said and did. If it does not measure up, it is not truth. He is the truth. God, in Christ, communicated His mind to man. That is, His truth was mediated through Him.

Jesus Christ and God's Truth

Now what has this to do with the slogan under review? Everything. "God's truth" is expressed in Jesus Christ. If "All truth" is to be found, therefore, it must be found in Him. He is the "Way" to God, the "Life" that He brings to those dead in trespasses and sins, and "the Truth" that communicates God's will to man (John 14:6). All truth is to be found in Him because there is no other source. That is why "All Truth[3] is God's Truth."

Moreover, if a "Truth" is "God's Truth," it cannot exist except in relationship to Him. For one to claim that a datum is from God he must show that it is intimately bound up with the thought of God; that it corresponds exactly to His way of seeing and interpreting the universe. Truth, therefore, cannot be established to be Truth apart from such a demonstration. It does not exist abstractly on its own; as the slogan faithfully expresses it, Truth is a relational thing. It is bound up with God's mind. But how can one demonstrate that any given datum out of the many data that exist is really God's Truth? It is not enough to assert it, he must show that this is fact. We shall come to that question presently, but for now, let's think a bit more about God's "Truth."

While God knows about every error imaginable, what He thinks about things is true – even what He thinks about error. All Truth resides in Him. Man, in his sinful nature, is prone to error. Since this is the case, he is not, and cannot, be the source of Truth.[4] Even before the fall, it was necessary for God to communicate facts to him and to issue commands. Man, at his best, was never able to generate Truth. He was created dependent upon God for it. So because "All Truth" comes from Him it is therefore "God's Truth."

---

3 Note that I have capitalized the word "Truth" (from this point on) since God expressed it by and in Jesus.
4 God says "For My thoughts are not your thoughts, Nor are your ways My ways …" (Isaiah 55:8, NASB).

Comprehensive Knowledge Necessary

Truth is the way that God sees things. In its communication, it is given in the way that God determined to communicate His thinking to men. But is that possible? God's knowledge is comprehensive. He knows all things. And He knows each of them in relation to all other things. Man's grasp on Truth – though in part communicated to him by God – can never be comprehensive. He can neither know all things nor how all things relate to one another. How, then, can man really know Truth?

The problem is this: since God's Truth has arisen from His comprehensive knowledge of all things, how can man ever be sure that he has Truth? Surely, he doesn't possess such vast knowledge. Yet without it, what seems to him to be true might no longer be so viewed if he were in possession of more pieces of the whole in their proper relations toward all other things, as God is. Then he might see things quite differently. Indeed, he might declare what he previously thought true, "false."

This is a problem that God solved in sending us the Truth, Jesus Christ. It is in Him that Truth can be known. It is necessary for man to have a Word from God in order to know what God's mind is. But again, if Christ is the Truth, how may one glean Truth from Him? And even if He is God's Word to man, how is sinful, limited, finite man to receive and assimilate the Truth God reveals since he does not possess comprehensive, unlimited knowledge? If he attains to any one part of it, isn't there a danger that he will not see things as God does because of his limitations by creation and further limitations due to sin? Then, would it still be Truth? Unless he is able to know all things in relationship to all other things (as God is), even if he has certain fragmented data from God, will he not distort them because of this fact? How can he help doing so when his knowledge is partial and not comprehensive? Doesn't comprehensive knowledge alone afford genuine Truth – the whole Truth, and nothing but the Truth? Again, in time, we shall take up this thorny matter. For now, simply think about the problem a bit. Epistemology[5] is central to the issues connected with obtaining Truth. Can you imagine what the solution to this problem is?

---

5 The study of how we know what we know.

Chapter Two

Since Truth *is* God's Truth…

Think of the Implications!

So far, we have seen how admirably the slogan "All Truth is God's Truth" expresses the biblical view of Truth. There can be no Truth apart from the One Who is *the* Truth, Jesus Christ. In word, in deed, and in attitude He is the standard of Truth; everything that purports to be "God's Truth" must conform to Him. His words and actions and attitudes alone are able to make God's inerrant Truth known to sinful men.

But we ran into some problems as well. We have yet to show how it is that God's Truth in Jesus becomes accessible to man and how when man receives a portion of it he can understand it properly, since he does not have comprehensive knowledge. It is possible, we suggested, that partial knowledge of Truth, and not the whole Truth, might lead him astray. So how can we overcome our limitations? These are important questions that we are leaving for further discussion at a later point in the book.

No Errors in God's Truth

For now, let us consider the slogan a bit further. God's Truth, like the Word of His Son in Whom it is embodied, is inerrant (as I indicated above). There are no errors, no fallacies, no faults in God's thinking or in its communication. He is always right, always truthful. That means that what He communicates to man is also entirely truthful; it contains no errors. And as the slogan reminds us, *all* Truth (not just some of it) is God's inerrant Truth. That means that whatever we accept as true for valid biblical reasons, we must also consider *wholly* true. Otherwise, it could not be called "God's Truth."

If you think certain data *may* be true, when they are only partially so, can they still be called God's Truth? Certainly not. Error mixed with Truth so contaminates absolute Truth that it no longer has the character of Truth. It has become error. The devil quoted Scripture, but added his word so that it became anything but God's Truth. The Pharisees possessed much scriptural Truth from God, but because of their misunderstandings, their misinterpretations, and their misrepresentations, they "annulled" God's Word (Matthew 15:6). What they believed and taught, though mixed with much Truth, was no longer God's Truth. An admixture of Truth and error can no longer be called "God's Truth." Like oil and water, the two do not adhere. Indeed, like similar poles of a magnet, they repel one another. They are utterly contradictory. Indeed, contaminated "truth" may be the most dangerous of all error since it often appears as if it were still God's Truth. So "all Truth" must be understood as meaning that Truth is, in every respect, "Truth"; no portion of it may be anything else.

Truth Must Not be Altered

In addition, God's Truth is unchangeable. It is not subject to modification, to alteration, to substitution, or to deletion. The Spirit caused the apostle John to write

> To all who hear the words of the prophecy of this scroll I testify this: If anybody adds to them God will add to him the plagues that are written in this scroll, and if anybody takes away from the words of the scroll of this prophecy God will take away his part from the tree of

life and from the holy city which are described in this scroll (Revelation 22:18, 19).

It is obvious from these words that God is deeply concerned about any alteration of His words. To do so carries heavy penalties. People must not call something purporting to be from Him "God's Truth" when it is some substitute for or alteration of the Truth as God gave it!

God Deals with those Who Distort Truth

An indication that God is concerned to have His people become certain that what is spoken is truly from Him may be found in His scathing words about the false prophets and those who listened to them in Jeremiah's day. He speaks of delivering His people into the hands of Nebuchadnezzar, the king of Babylon, because they listened to Ahab and Zedekiah whom, He said, were "prophesying to you falsely in My name ... he [the Babylonian king] shall slay them before your eyes" (Jeremiah 29:21, NASB). If you wish to read more about this matter of falsely prophesying in God's Name, read the twenty-seventh chapter of Jeremiah or the thirteenth chapter of Ezekiel. It is serious business to say that something is God's Truth when it is not. So, those who use the slogan must be cautious. They must be certain that what they call God's Truth really is so. One can only regret that from time to time it seems that many declare that something is "God's truth" without measuring it alongside the One Who is the Truth. And in an all too casual manner, some declare that those who do not accept their views as from God are simply denying that all truth is God's Truth. Care must always be taken when saying that something is God's Truth that, indeed, it is in complete harmony with His Word. As Jeremiah indicates, both those who falsely claim their word is God's, *and those who listen to them,* will end in calamity.

Error is Rife

So it is enormously important to be certain you are *properly* reporting that a recommended belief, attitude, or action is from God before asking others to accept, assimilate, and follow it. There has been much error spread abroad among God's people throughout the ages, and God has always contested it in the strongest terms. Many of the books of the New Testament were written in large measure to clarify what God actually said rather than that which others falsely claimed was His Truth. The Scriptures clearly show that all who teach and all who follow false teaching are in danger of misrepresenting God's will to the peril of both. Because it is a grave matter to say (intentionally or otherwise) that something is "God's Truth" when it is not, God holds those who teach error responsible. They will receive a two-fold judgment; they misrepresent God and they mislead His people. James writes, "My brothers, not many of you should become teachers, because you know that we teachers will receive stricter judgment" (James 3:1). It is vital, then, to know that you are not bringing down judgment upon yourself by falsely attributing something to God which is not from Him. At the outset of this chapter, I referred to the implications of the fact that "All Truth *is* God's Truth." Perhaps considering the *implications* of asserting that something is His Truth when it isn't may make you more hesitant about using the slogan to cover data that you know only *may* (or possibly may *not*) actually be God's Truth.

Chapter Three

Solving the Problems

Problems Summarized

As you doubtless remember, I left some matters hanging, while promising to deal with them in time. Now is the time. To recapitulate:

1. I asserted that Jesus, God's Word to man, is the only source of God's Truth and asked how you and I may appropriate it.

2. I also posed the question that if we must have comprehensive knowledge to keep from contaminating God's Truth, how can we sinners do so with all of our limitations?

I want to address both of those matters in this chapter.

Acquisition of Truth

First, how may one acquire God's Truth? The answer is: from His written Word, which exactly approximates the living Word Who became flesh. This is a simple answer that I shall elucidate later in the chapter. "But," you ask, "how can we keep from contaminating scriptural Truth by our faulty partial understandings of it, by our sinful biases, and by our creaturely limitations? After all, we don't have the whole picture." I want to respond to that second question first, but in doing so I shall find it necessary to interrelate both questions.

Even though God's Truth as presented in the Bible is wholly true because the Bible is God's inerrant revelation which issued forth from His absolute, comprehensive knowledge of all things past, present, and future, including the exact relationships of these things to each other, it is still possible to learn from the Scriptures what God has said in a "truly" truthful way. Since we lack divine attributes we are caught up in our sinful biases, our finite limitations, and our partial knowledge. Doesn't it follow, then, that we will contaminate God's Truth by those attributes which characterize us? Yes, it does – unless some third factor is present to make it possible to glean God's Truth truly in spite of our finitude and propensity to error. How is that?

What the Scriptures Say

To begin with, notice that the Bible itself affirms that it is the trustworthy, dependable, unchangeable Word of God from which believers may learn God's Truth. The Psalmist declares, "Through Your precepts I get understanding; Therefore, I hate every false way" (Psalm 119:104). *How* can that be so? That, of course, is not the principal question. Even if we were not able to understand how sinful, finite man can "get understanding" of God's Truth, it is important to believe that it is possible. He says so. After all, the very presence of such a book addressed to mankind which, as it does, purports to reveal all the Truth that is needed to love God and one's neighbor, attests to the fact that God intended for His children to understand that Truth. But again, how can sinful, finite man do so? First, notice the utter reliability of the perfect, far-reaching nature of God's written revelation. Apart from such dependability, understanding of Truth would be impossible.

Listen to the same writer facing the fact that God's Truth is comprehensive and absolute: "Forever, Yahweh, Your Word is settled in heaven" (Psalm 119:89). That is crucial. Unlike science, which constantly changes since no absolute Truth is found in it, there is no need for God to correct or modify His Word once it is written.[6] Over the years, more and more revelation was forthcoming from God until the Bible was complete, but none of what God revealed later on changed what went before so that it was necessary to declare that earlier revelations were in error. Science, not being "settled in heaven," can't boast the same. God's Word alone is totally reliable. That makes it certain that from its pages one may obtain a portion of absolute Truth.

To continue, note that in verse 96 the writer says, "I have seen an end to all perfection; Your commandment is exceedingly broad." No other claims to perfection – even about delicate technological instruments in a "clean room" – hold up. All created elements have their limits – and faults. Perfection is not found in man or in the products of his hands. Yet, God's perfect Word is "broad." That means that its scope is beyond our unaided ability to grasp. It covers all the territory that could ever concern us; it is sufficient for life and godliness (cf. II Peter 1:3).

The Answer

So then, it is possible to learn Truth "truthfully" from the Bible so that it becomes "a lamp to [one's] feet And a light to [his] path" (v. 105). That is to say, God's Truth may be acquired from the Scriptures and assimilated by God's children so as to use it in practical, day by day living. But again, how is this possible? This same Psalmist continually answers that question. For instance, he asks God, "Open my eyes that I may behold wonderful things out of Your law" (v. 18).[7] Recognizing that in His own limited ability he is unable to rightly extract and apply God's Truth, he calls for help. Again, we encounter the same plea: "Make me understand

---

6   Incidentally, this "settled" condition is antithetical to "Open Theology" in which God changes His mind and His ways in response to what man does.

7   His problem was not eyesight but insight. Under the former metaphor he expresses his need for divine assistance in interpreting Scripture.

the way of Your precepts, and I will meditate on Your wonders" (v. 27). He realizes that if he is to understand the Bible, God Himself must enable him to do so. Elsewhere, he calls upon God to be his Bible Teacher: "Yahweh, teach me the way of Your statutes, and I will keep it to the end" (v. 33). He recognizes that he cannot live according to Scripture unless God first teaches him the meaning of passages which show him how to walk in a godly manner. In the following verse (v. 34) he reiterates his desire: "Make me understand and I will keep Your law and observe it with my whole heart." Unless God causes him to understand the Word that He has given, he will not be able to observe it. And, finally, think about verse 73, "Your hands have made me and formed me; give me discernment that I may learn Your commandments." He who calls upon His Creator for help knows his creaturely limitations.

Divine Help Available

In each of these quotations from Psalm 119, which in every verse speaks about the Bible, the writer finds it imperative to call upon his God to enable him to understand and appropriate it. This constant refrain makes it quite evident that the way in which sinful, finite man is able to interpret the Bible so as to properly understand what the revealed Truth of God has to say is by God's help in response to prayer. Man is limited, man is biased but, in spite of that, the Holy Spirit, Who caused the Bible to be written, enables him to correctly interpret and use it in order to please God. That is why Jesus called Him the "Spirit of Truth" (John 14:17): He "moved" the biblical writers to pen Truth and He enables us to read and apply Truth. Apart from His help, we would distort the Truth. Who better understands the Bible than its divine Author?

So what do we have in God's providence? We have an inerrant "Word of Truth" from Him.[8] Out of His comprehensive knowledge, He has selected those data that He knows we need to

---
8 I have not taken space to argue for inerrancy; I assume that those who read believe it.

please and serve Him, and He has sent His Spirit to enable us to rightly understand His Truth and empower us to live according to it.[9] Now, those are significant factors in solving problems so as to live a godly life. No wonder Paul wrote,

> Who knows the thoughts of a person except the spirit of the person in him; so too no one knows God's thoughts except God's Spirit. Now we haven't received the world's spirit but the Spirit Who is from God, so that we may know that which God has freely given to us. ... Who has known the Lord's mind; who will instruct Him? But we have the mind of Christ (I Corinthians 2:11, 12, 16).

Paul was talking about understanding the "teachings of God's Spirit" (v. 14). Jesus said, "knowledge about the secrets of the kingdom from the heavens has been given to you, and it hasn't been given to them" (Matthew 13:11). Since the regenerate man has the Spirit dwelling within him, he has "the mind of Christ." So, as important as it is to say "Your law is truth" (Psalm 119:142), unless God causes us to understand what we read, it would be quite unprofitable. But praise Him, He has made provision for us to acquire and assimilate Truth (I Corinthians 2:9, 10).

So both questions have been answered in discussing the second one. We are able to know Truth, because God has from His infinite knowledge and wisdom, selected portions of His comprehensive knowledge of Truth and deposited them in the Bible. And, lest our limitations keep us from understanding those portions of eternal Truth that He purposed to give us, He has provided the Holy Spirit to enable us to do so. The Spirit always interprets correctly, since He knows the thoughts of God and, by indwelling us, causes us to think, understand, and apply God's Truth as if we had the actual "mind of Christ."

---

9 Cf. Colossians 1:9–11; Ephesians 1:15–20; Hebrews 13:20, 21.

Solving the Problems

What a wonderful thing! We have a revelation from God which we can utterly depend upon. And when we ask Him in faith, God enables us to correctly interpret His Word so as to understand that portion of Truth *as He does*. Though we do not have comprehensive knowledge, nevertheless, we do have the benefit of it. With the Psalmist let us exclaim, "Your Word has been tested and found to be very pure; Therefore, Your servant loves it!" (Psalm 119:140). How can we mere creatures, whom He has redeemed by the death and resurrection of His Son, dare to mix the "very pure" Word of Truth with the never pure (at its best) word of man?

Chapter Four

Serious Matters

So we have seen that God's Truth is communicated through His written Word just as through the living Word. And we have learned that the only way to avoid contaminating that Word with our limited ideas and falsehoods is to never attempt to integrate the two but, instead, to seek God's help in interpreting and applying the Truth. Moreover, we are aware of the fact that God does not look kindly upon those who claim to speak for Him when what they teach is something else. False teaching may be knowingly or unknowingly set forth as if it were God's Truth (sometimes combining Truth with error). Either way, the one who teaches it and those who listen to him are engaging in serious defection from the Truth.

Danger! A Sweet Tooth for Error

Because, as the Pharisees demonstrated (as well as the devil before them), it is possible to clothe error in the garments of Truth by mishandling and misrepresenting God's Word. Like poison administered to an unsuspecting victim, error is often embedded in something sweet that looks and tastes like Truth. This makes error desirable (cf. Genesis 3:1). Christians who listen to those who purport to teach biblical Truth, then, must not take what they hear at face value but, like the Bereans, they must check it out by intensively studying the Bible for themselves to determine its truthfulness (Acts 17:11).[10]

Now as we have seen, the Holy Spirit respects the power of His Word to change people and helps those Christians who sincerely want to know and teach God's Truth. It is true that the biblical Word never returns void, but always accomplishes what God intended it to accomplish through the working of His providence (cf. Isaiah 55:11), but that in no way removes the responsibility of exerting personal effort in the study of the Bible. Biblical interpreters must call upon God's help, taking full responsibility for any failure to do so. After all, this is no minor matter; God's Word is called "the Word of Truth"! As we have seen, it is not to be handled lightly. Listen to Paul's full statement of the matter:

> Do your best to present yourself to God tried and true, a workman who won't be ashamed, cutting the Word of Truth with accuracy (II Timothy 2:15).

The workman in the Word is like a carpenter or stone mason who must cut one stone or board to fit exactly to another. So as one ministers the Word of God, he must cut it so as to make Truth accurately fit each one he addresses. Dependence upon the Spirit to enable you to interpret and minister the Word is crucial because God will shame you if you do not depend on Him.[11] The Bible contains a large number of warnings about the misuse of the Scriptures (I have mentioned but a few). That is because of the tendency of sinful men – ever since the Garden of Eden – to listen to the Devil's lies, and then justify their acceptance by distorting

---

10 By "intensive study" I refer to how the Bereans examined the Scriptures daily to discover whether what Paul taught was Truth or error. If Luke commends their scrutiny of Paul's teaching, surely we ought to be as diligent in examining the teaching of others. Intensive study, however, implies that a person knows how to do so. My book, *What to Do on Thursday*, provides practical help in learning how to interpret, apply, and appropriate Scripture.

11 For more about this, see my book, *Committed to Craftsmanship*.

the Truth. Often, as in the case of Adam and Eve, this distortion takes place when people want something that he offers that they (wrongly) think will be to their advantage.

Truth in Counseling

One of the principal areas in which exegetical violations take place is in the practice of counseling. Here, I am not thinking so much of contaminating God's Truth by trying to amalgamate it with human error, as of the unintentional misuse of Scripture to justify teaching which does not come from the Bible and is antithetical to it. Often, this takes place as a teacher misuses the Bible to propagate the blatant falsehood that amalgamation in no way contaminates Truth. Those who want to bolster eclectic theories and practices are prone to do this. Here are a few examples (selected at random from a host of others) of what I am talking about. Notice how Scripture is "used" to justify non-scriptural doctrine.

Misusing Scripture

In his book, *Self Esteem: You're Better Than You Think*, Ray Burwick uses Romans 12:2 to support his mistaken understanding of Paul's words,

> Don't be conformed to the way of our modern age, but be transformed by the renewal of your mind, so that you may be able to determine what God's good and pleasing and perfect will is …

to mean that "You don't have to be enslaved by a poor self-image."[12] If this verse means anything, it means that one must be careful not to go on following the views of the age (e.g., self-esteem doctrine) but, instead, to have his thinking renewed so as to discover God's will from God's Word, by means of which the renewal of the mind takes place. Paul wants the believer to learn God's perfect will in contrast to the teachings of the world.

---

12 Tyndale House: Wheaton: 1983, p. 55.

Larry Crabb uses Romans 1:21 to attempt to undergird his Adlerian view of the need for security and significance. He writes, "By not bowing the knee to God's purposes and lordship, they lost all hope of true significance ... they struck out on their own, thus giving up any real security."[13] Crabb is reaching! To endeavor to find the Adlerian teaching of man's "need" for security and significance, in a passage explaining the sins of the Gentiles and God's judgment upon them, clearly shows the desperation of one who "had to" discover this teaching "somewhere" in the Bible – even though it is not there. The passage, in conjunction with what Paul wrote in chapters two and three, if anything, should lead men to repentance and faith, not to a sense of their significance!

Selwyn Hughes says that Proverbs 23:7 ("As he thinks in his heart, so is he," NKJV) refers to "distortions of reality based on faulty and erroneous thinking."[14] In order to find support for Albert Ellis' pagan view of man and his needs, he distorts the verse from Proverbs. This faulty use of the Proverb may have resulted from his failure to exegete the passage carefully, possibly through ignorance (which is not excusable – he is teaching others, remember). Of course, as the context of the verse shows (and this is one of the few verses in Proverbs from Chapter 10 on that appears in a context), the writer refers to words spoken when offering food that do not represent the inner thoughts of the speaker's heart. The verse is talking about hypocrisy. As any modern translation plainly shows, this is clear from the context.[15]

Astonishingly, the very slogan we have been considering is often paraded forth as justification for the contaminating and distorting beliefs and procedures that eclectic integrationists

---

13 *Effective Biblical Counseling*, Zondervan: Grand Rapids (1977), p. 72.
14 *Helping People Through Their Problems*, Bethany House: Minneapolis (1981), p. 92.
15 See for instance, my translation of Proverbs 23:6–8 in the *Christian Counselor's Commentary Series*.

practice. As we have seen, the slogan prohibits any such thing. Yet Carter and Narramore confidently say,

> All truth is God's truth. Consequently, the truths of psychology are not contradictory to the truths of divine revelation; in fact, they have the potential of being integrated into a harmonious whole.[16]

They do not demonstrate that psychology can discover any "truths," nor could they ever claim such "truths" to be divinely given. Their confidence, as we shall see, is based upon a theory of revelation which is untenable. Many unsuspecting Christians have been lured into accepting the fallacious view that since all Truth is God's Truth, it is perfectly acceptable to look for God's Truth in the writings of unbelieving psychologists and psychiatrists.

Unsuspecting Christians, who are led astray by the supposed "consequence" of such teaching, have no reticence about sending their loved ones and parishioners to eclectic (or unbelieving) counselors, and some go on to become such counselors themselves. This sad situation actually involves a bald denial of the slogan which eclectic counselors wave as their banner.

Assertion Not Enough

The mere assertion of the slogan to justify the adoption of viewpoints and methods of sinful, limited, human counselors is not sufficient. Indeed, it is woefully inadequate. Yet in the quotation above, the writers assume that the statement "consequently" leads to integration. As a matter of fact, we have seen that it does just the opposite. They cannot demonstrate that their proposition is correct without misusing the Scriptures. By avoiding the standards set forth in the Bible and by setting up their own in an autonomous manner, they have made themselves the standard by which they think and act. The slogan, wrongly interpreted, becomes their

---

16 John Carter and Bruce Narramore, *The Integration of Theology and Psychology*. Zondervan: Grand Rapids (1980), p. 49.

standard. They say, "All truth is God's truth. Consequently…" Do you see how even a slogan that, rightly interpreted, is in line with Scripture and opposed to integration, may be used to teach against what the Bible says? This is not the whole of their book, of course, but it does indicate the sort of reasoning that is found in it.

The Source of Error

Integrationists rarely (if ever) consider the corollary to the slogan: "All error is the Devil's error." The question to be asked of those who purport to glean God's Truth from a human source, in addition to the Bible, is "How do you distinguish God's Truth from the Devil's Error?" The only valid answer for a Christian is "By means of comparing data with what the Scriptures teach." But if the Bible, as they think, is insufficient to reveal all the Truth necessary to do counseling, how is it to become a standard of that which it fails to set forth? It may be delinquent in the very areas that are being questioned. In other words, for integrationists, the Bible is not sufficient. It is only possibly helpful. Beyond that, the determination as to what is Truth or error is made by the integrationist himself. While he ought to turn to the Bible as the standard, his position forces him to turn to his own opinions instead. When he becomes his own standard, that is sinful autonomy!

If the Bible is the standard of Truth, then it must not be commingled with anything else. Upon mixing of the divine Word with the human word all becomes indistinct. Everything grows cloudy – all certainty is lost. The standard has been so weakened by the commingling process that the thinking Christian must conclude that this approach leaves him with no way of distinguishing God's Truth from the Devil's error.

Chapter Five

Revelation

"Perhaps," you say, "there is nothing more to discuss." I agree; there shouldn't be. But I wish it were that easy to convince the integrationists. Hence, it will be necessary to consider their views more fully.

General Revelation for Counseling?

They are clear about one thing: they believe that psychological "truths" have been revealed by God. How can they say so? By appealing to the category of "General Revelation." For instance, here is what an integrationist, J. Harold Ellens, said when writing about me: "He apparently never even thought of the notion that all truth as God's truth, has equal warrant, whether truth from nature or scripture."[17] The error in his statement as regards me is of no consequence. It just shows how little some writers know about Nouthetic Counseling. What is important is his comment that truth from nature and Scripture have "equal warrant." It is this sort of thinking with which we shall be concerned in the present chapter. Ellens is not alone. Both he and William F. English think

---

17 In Douglas Bookman, *The Scriptures and Biblical Counseling*, John MacArthur and Wayne Mack, *Introduction to Biblical Counseling*. Word: Dallas (1994), p. 71. Bookman retorts, "Such a charge is simply ludicrous. Adams has written at copious lengths about this specific issue." He is, of course, correct and Ellens is wrong.

that God reveals truth through "nature," or General Revelation. But listen to English: "Truth derived from the study of any segment of general revelation, whether psychology, or any other field, is not as trustworthy as the truth found in the Scriptures"[18] Two problems arise as we consider these statements.

They differ from the Christian view at a crucial point: is truth really Truth? Ellens thinks so, referring to the slogan we have been considering and calling the supposed "truth" derived from General Revelation Truth. For him, therefore, psychological truth is "God's Truth." One can only wonder at the thinking of English at this point when he too speaks of "truth derived from ... general revelation," which is "not as trustworthy as the truth found in the Scriptures." He proposes, therefore, the "filtering" of "psychological truth through biblical truth."

Is "truth" Truth?

What is truth for English? How can anyone think that "truth" may be untrustworthy – especially if he adheres to the slogan, "All truth is God's truth"? Truth is Truth. If it is God's Truth given by General Revelation, then it cannot be considered as less "trustworthy" than His Truth given in Special Revelation (the Bible). How can any truth be more or less "trustworthy and still be God's Truth?" All of God's Truth is trustworthy. And if the Truth derived from General Revelation is from God, how can one speak of filtering it? You can't filter out error from God's Truth because in His Truth there is none! Truth is Truth – but English doesn't seem to think so. He has two kinds of "truth."[19] How can there be such? What does he mean by less trustworthy truth? If it is less

---

18 Ibid., p. 91.
19 Cf. H. Newton Malony's analysis of Gary Collins' view: "He distinguishes 'TRUTH' from 'truth,' and recognizes that because the various data under examination are from different sources (some revealed and some empirically derived), tension is bound to exist between Christian and non-Christian (continued on the next page)

trustworthy, but still God's Truth, then God's Word (at least in part) is untrustworthy. How can this be? The sloppy thinking that is often found in the integrationist movement makes it difficult to critique. Truth, if it "truly" is Truth, is always trustworthy – simply because it is Truth.

What "truth"?

There are many non-Christians who talk of truth as if every man has his own truth. While I am sure that English does not believe this, it is necessary to warn those who read him of the danger of this sort of speaking because it can easily lead to thinking the way these unbelievers do. When he says that truth must be "filtered," he cannot possibly mean that such truth is Truth; otherwise it could not be called truth – could it? You don't filter truth in order to obtain the truth that is within truth. The language used is patently ridiculous.

What he seems to be trying to say (however badly) is that non-truth has been mixed with Truth (that supposedly comes from God in General Revelation) and must be filtered out of the mix. But his words seem to say that truths mixed with lesser truths have to be separated. The difficulty that he has is simply this: he has called General Revelation a source of "psychological truth," but he can't bring himself to believe that General Revelation is really Revelation. And that is the crux of the matter.

Is General Revelation Really "Revelation"?

Is the so-called psychological "truth" that one finds in nature revelation? To appeal to "General Revelation," as most integrationists do in order to enhance the credibility of their theories, raises serious questions. As English's words indicate, this is a slippery thing to get hold of. It is almost like those who speak

---

psychologists." Collins and Malony, *Psychology and Theology, Prospects for Integration*. Abingdon: Nashville (1981), p. 90.

of mental illness, sometimes stressing the word "illness" in order to snatch a counselee away from biblical counselors and, at other times, stressing the word "mental" whenever they wish to say that they should counsel him instead of sending him to a physician. I once spoke at the Rosemead Graduate School and, in the question-and-answer session that followed, an attendee said "You can't deal with persons who are mentally ill." My reply to this psychologist (who evidently thought the "mentally ill" were in his domain) was, "Neither can you if they are truly ill! Psychologists are not doctors either." Sometimes such people find it convenient to stress one thing, sometimes another.

Now something of that sort happens when integrationists speak of revelation and of something less trustworthy. English has called the something-less-than-trustworthy material revelation; others, more astute, find it necessary to do something else, when convenient. But when these same people want to gain credibility for their views, they speak of this material as revelation from God which has "equal warrant" with biblical Truth.

The confusion over these matters is obvious. But that confusion is endemic to integrationism. That is because they try but "can't have it both ways," as the saying goes. Either General Revelation is truly revelation, or it isn't. If it is revelation, clearly there is nothing to filter. It is all as pure as the words of Scripture (Special Revelation).

Where is the "truth"?

All revelation from God is inerrant. This fact poses a new problem for the integrationist. He can call some theory, idea, or method supposedly discovered in nature "God's Truth" if he wishes, but if he thinks for a minute, how is he to establish it as such? In no other field of endeavor has there been so much disagreement. Psychologists retool throughout their lifetime to keep up with the latest newly-uncovered system (or parts thereof). Think of all those systems that were once called God's Truth that have been discarded![20] Gary Almy, MD, remarks, "Lacking solid foundation, one movement after another has come and gone over the course of psychotherapy's one-hundred-year history."[21] Others, tired of the retooling process, cling to one or another outmoded or debunked system. How could this be true if any were "psychological truth" that has been revealed? Which theory is True and which is not? Why should there be a mixture of truth and error if God has truly revealed Truth? Did God want to confuse us? Revelation, whether General or Special, is always inerrant. In Special Revelation, we can turn with confidence to any part of it and be sure that we are dealing with Truth. In dealing with nature, on the other hand, integrationists tell us that we must separate truth from error, revealed materials from

---

20 The situation is almost as bad as faddish nutritional and health advice. Views change with the next article you read. What should one believe? In the *Spartanburg Herald Journal* this humorous article which sets up the problem appeared: "The Japanese eat very little fat and suffer fewer heart attacks than the British and Americans. The French eat a lot of fat and also suffer fewer heart attacks than the British or Americans. The Japanese drink very little red wine and suffer fewer heart attacks than the British or Americans. The Italians drink excessive amounts of red wine and suffer fewer heart attacks than the British or Americans. In conclusion, eat and drink what you like. Speaking English apparently is what kills you."
William L. Isley, MD, writes: "The medical literature contains thousands of articles which have now been corrected, disregarded or even have been shown to be flagrantly wrong despite the presence of a "statistically significant *p* value for the results" (*The Journal of Biblical Ethics in Medicine, Vol. 5, No 4.* pp.65, 66).

21 Gary Almy, *How Christian is Christian Counseling?* Crossway: Wheaton (2000), p. 241. Almy continues: "It is characteristic of the history of psychotherapy that new ideas constantly push old ones from the scene. ... Before the Recovery Memory Therapy movement of the mid 1980s, one version of psychotherapy after another had come and gone in faddish ways" (pp. 244, 248).

non-revealed materials. If there were Truth mixed with error, who gets to decide what is revelation and what is not?

What Psychology is "True"?

There is trouble in River City! Psychology, thought of as a science, must agree with science's fundamental premise that nothing is final, all is in flux. What today is considered a fact, tomorrow is rejected as disproved. This is true of many once-cherished views. Once people believed in the Phlogiston theory of negative weight. Bringing this concept into some mathematical equations helped them explain facts having to do with the weight of burned substances before and after the burning process. Since then it has been held that in burning, something also enters into the material burned, thus causing the residue to be heavier than before burning. Who knows whether or not there will be a later modification of this view? Science changes precisely because, unlike revelation, there is no assurance that what it learns is Truth.

All Truth is Truth. Whatever Truth is revealed in General Revelation must therefore be true – not partially so, or even mostly so. To say otherwise is to say that, in nature, God gave us contaminated truth, or no truth at all. Neither can be correct. Revelation from God is always wholly true. But what truth is revealed through General Revelation? Is it truth about automobile mechanics? About medicine (think of the changes in that field!)? About cooking? Or biology, or – you name it! Why should psychology be any different? Indeed, there is no proof that psychology – in any of its parts – has been revealed.

And if it were true that General Revelation may be found in psychology, we must ask what psychology? As has been observed, there are more than 250 differing psychological systems abroad in this country alone, each competing for recognition as the true one. What proliferation! And who is able in one lifetime to read, understand, and evaluate all of them? There is only one Bible;

there are multiple psychologies. Who is to say that any given psychotherapist's system is correct and that it should be imposed upon others? Indeed, to say so, in the face of the unparalleled proliferation of theories, is sheer arrogance. He who affirms this has made himself the standard of truth for everyone else! Yet, if his discoveries were true revelation, he should do that very thing.

Common Grace

There is no question, then, that the psychologist who wants to claim that what he accepts is truth because it has been revealed by God in nature is in a peck of trouble. But to this is added the notion of "common grace." By that designation, God is supposed to have graciously given truth to all men alike. But is there not a problem there also? Certainly, in His grace, God does good to all men. In spite of their sin, He restrains them from becoming as bad as they might and enables them in part to discover facts about the world in which they live. But these discoveries are distorted by man's limitations and rebellion, and are certainly not inerrant or inspired, as revelation always is.

Does God expect all men to be able to understand His book of nature, without distortion, any more than they understand His book of Special Revelation? Indeed, all that we know that God revealed in creation is that He is a good and powerful Creator Who will hold men responsible (see Romans 1; Psalm 19). He didn't reveal the elements of science – or of psychology. There is nothing in the Bible about revealing psychological truth through General Revelation. The Bible looks on General Revelation as limited to non-salvific information about the existence of a good Creator. And even this minimal amount of revelation is suppressed by sinful man (Romans 1:18; cf. also vv. 21–27). Since that is the fact, of what value can psychological theories be? In the eyes of many Christians who are psychologists, "'Natural revelation' [which integrationists fall back on to justify their position] has not supplemented the Bible, but supplanted it in many areas."[22]

Revelation is from God

Revelation then – all of it, so long as it is information truly revealed by God – is inerrant. Nothing else can be said to be inerrant, except that sort of general (non-specific) revelation of God as the Creator of man and things who holds us responsible for knowing that which is found in the "book of nature." Indeed, it is entirely false to speak of what science discovers as divine *revelation*. It is human *discovery* made possible by common grace – and that is all. Revelation comes from God; discovery from man. And the discoveries that are unearthed may or may not be correctly interpreted. Most of the supposed "discoveries" turn out to be nothing more than the views of humans trying to understand nature. Surely this cannot be rightly termed "revelation."

It is necessary to recognize, then, that the "facts" unearthed are man's discoveries, not God's revelation. Discoveries come from man at work in his world; revelation comes from God at work in His world. The great difference between revelation and discovery, I repeat, is that the former is always from God; the latter is not.

Having explored this matter somewhat cursorily, I shall now look at some of the supposed "revelations" of psychology.

---

22 Isley, op. cit., p. 66. Brackets mine.

Chapter Six

No Consensus

Consider carefully these words of H. Newton Malony:

> However, it is not very helpful to speak of God as the source of all truth, if the truth that comes from God through the Bible is differentiated from the truth that comes from either psychology or Anthropology.[23]

He couldn't be more correct. He is criticizing Collins' view of "integration" when writing this. He has noted one of Collins' principal failures in his attempt to integrate psychology and Christianity. We shall not go into Malony's liberal view of the Scriptures, since that would take us too far afield. But, as Collins properly says in a rejoinder to Malony, "To me, this sounds like a popular theological view that sees revelation located in events and experiences, but not in the words of the Bible."[24] Collins in this rebuttal is also correct. But the basic integrationist positions of both are wrong![25]

---

23 Op. cit., p. 88. Gary Collins has been at the head of the integrationist movement.
24 Ibid., p. 131.
25 It is sad, but amusing, that the integrationists can't even agree about how to integrate!

Collins's View Typical

Collins, with many others in his camp, thinks that psychological data are revealed through General Revelation. He speaks of "the benefits of God's natural revelation as revealed in psychology" [emphasis mine].[26] But so far as the Bible is concerned, what General Revelation[27] tells us is explained in Psalm 19, Romans 1, and similar passages. In no place is General Revelation represented as providing more than knowledge about the glory of a great Creator Who is powerful, and with Whom man is in trouble. There is no reason to think that any "discoveries" of psychology, therefore, are revelation. The notion is foreign to the Scriptures.

All Revelation Inerrant

As I have pointed out earlier, all true *revelation* is inerrant. Creation truthfully, infallibly, reveals the basic facts about a Creator. God reveals no half truths, errors, nor anything else but pure Truth. Yet even Collins has to agree that discoveries in the field of psychology, unlike those Truths revealed in the Bible, are of a very different order. The one is perfect (as we have seen in an earlier chapter) while the other is riddled with error. To speak as Collins and many others do, of psychology as "revealed" is, therefore, a serious error. Probably, this mistaken and misleading terminology is but the result of shoddy theological thought, but it cannot be excused. "Why not give him a pass on this one?" you ask. Because this terminology greatly confuses the uninitiated. They are led to believe that God has two great books of revelation – nature and the Bible – that both are of the same nature and both on an equal level. But that is quite wrong. The two sources of revelation are from God, of course, but the nature of each is quite different: the one is verbal, propositional; the other is non-verbal. The one is revealed

---

26 Ibid. p. 59. Note the stress upon revelation. The word, it seems, is used to lend authority to the supposed discoveries of psychology.
27 Collins, here, calls it "natural revelation."

Truth about man, his problems and God's solution to them. The other says nothing about salvation or sanctification.

Flawed Thinking

To speak of the teachings of psychology as "revealed" truth, then, discloses seriously flawed thinking. Yet, that is precisely the position of Collins, who has been the leading light among integrationists:

> All truth is God's truth, therefore, the truths of psychology (general revelation) are neither contradictory nor contrary to revealed truth (special revelation) but are integrative in a harmonious whole.[28]

Clearly, he is hopelessly mixed up in the use of terminology or in his thinking – or both. How can Collins speak of the supposed "truths of psychology" as "revealed" through General *Revelation*, while at the same time, distinguishing the Truth which comes from Special Revelation (the Bible) from General Revelation by calling the former "revealed truth"? If the term "revealed truth" is what segregates the one from the other, then it is confusing for him to use the word "revelation" of both. If both are "revelation" are not both "revealed truth"? What Collins wants to do is put the two on a similar level, but in the attempt, contradicts himself. He wants presumed psychological discoveries (which certainly are *not* revealed truths) to be thought of as coming from God as biblical Truth does, so he speaks about these supposed "discoveries" under the rubric "revelation." As I said before, "You can't have it both ways!"

No Agreement

The history of counseling psychology makes one thing clear: nothing can be called "the assured results" of psychology. With at least 250 differing views in America today, the notion is ludicrous.

---

28   Ibid., p. 28.

No Consensus

In a court trial in San Diego's North County, of which I was the foreman, a forensic psychiatrist, Richard Rapport, was called to the stand. The astute assistant district attorney asked him "Do psychiatrists agree about anything?" Under oath, this well-known psychiatrist replied, "No." How, then, can Collins – or anyone else – speak of psychological ideas and dogmas as "revealed?" The notion is beyond reasonable belief! Think of the history of psychology: system after system from the late 1800s until today has been replaced by the next one. There have been the theories of Wundt, Titchener, James, Angell, Thorndike, Pavlov, Watson, Lashley, Cattell, Weiss, Hull, Freud, Rogers, Skinner, Wertheimer, Lewin, McDougal, Meyer, Adler, and Allport in the early years; and there has been an innumerable host of others since. These all found fault with one another's viewpoints which they sought to refine or replace. Obviously, there is no inerrant revelation to be obtained from them through so-called "Natural Revelation"! There is nothing but proliferation in this field; unlike nearly all other fields of endeavor, there is no consensus! Psychology is notorious for the lack of agreement among its practitioners.

It ought to be apparent that to even think of equating biblical Truth with "psychological truth" is nonsense. There is no similarity. Even if psychology were able to discover "God's truth" (which is always true, and never in error, remember), the results of the twentieth century demonstrate that psychologists have made a botch of the job. For the sake of the argument, even if one or another psychologist did happen to discover "God's truth" how would we know? Who would be able to extract that "truth" from the proliferation of views? After all, there are no signs and wonders to authenticate it or those who propagate it, as there were in the writing of the Scriptures.[29] When the psycho-biggies of 1981 met for the first time ever in a week-long conference in Phoenix, Arizona, their spokesperson who reported on the event in Time

---

29 See my book, *Signs and Wonders in the Last Days*.

magazine said that they "agreed on one thing only – that they agreed on nothing!" Is that God's Truth?

Now, you will notice that what psychologists come up with I have called supposed "discoveries," not truth – let alone "*God's* Truth." If they should "discover" absolute Truth, we'd never know it. But we have seen that is not possible for them to do so. The only Truth about man, his problems, and their solutions that may correctly be called "God's Truth" is that which He has inerrantly revealed in Scripture. All other ideas "discovered" are the result of human thought and activity. Psychotherapists whose erasers often wear down before their pencils do, by seeking to learn all they can about the world they live in, think that they can mine "God's Truth" from nature. But when it comes to "discovering" in nature what God has already revealed in the Bible, the attempt is worse than futile. It is unnecessary and misleading. We have seen how the only truly "revealed" facts about man and his condition must come from God in an *inerrant* manner. According to the disagreements among psychologists, on their own reading, there has been nothing but demonstrated error. The history of psychology shows that rather than agreement on Truth, there has been nothing but disagreement. Psychology possesses no revealed Truth other than that which has been borrowed from the Bible. Consequently, its additional "findings" will always be uncertain at best and, more likely, untrue.

The Bible in Contrast

"But wait a minute – what of your inerrant Bible?" someone asks. "It's no better. The Bible has spawned a group of discordant teachers, denominations, and the like. Christian 'Truth' can be no better than psychological 'truth,' then, can it?" This is an objection which warrants a serious reply. Here an important distinction must be made. Differing fallible human interpretations of that which is inerrant does not make the source less than inerrant. It remains the same. Psychology never had an inerrant source to begin with as the Christian theologian has. So as you see the differences among Christians, you must recognize two things:

1. Christian interpreters are one big step closer to infallible Truth. Psychology begins with the erroneous "discoveries" of men; Christianity begins with the inerrant revelation of God. That, in itself makes a huge difference.

2. Secondly, the differences among true Christians are minor. All agree on the fundamentals of the faith. The same cannot be said of the differences among psychologists. They differ not as Presbyterians and Baptists do, but as Christians and Muslims do. That is quite a difference! Because of that fact, later we shall have to look at some of the obvious errors that have been "discovered" by various schools of thought. These are "obvious" to any thinking Christian because they so clearly differ from the Scriptures. But first, let us consider the view of "two revelations" from another perspective.

Chapter Seven

Can You Call This "God's Truth"?

Common Territory

Because psychology attempts to cover the same area as the Bible does[30] – helping to change people so that they will love others and have peace and joy in their lives – how can they be described as two separate disciplines? Only by diminishing the Bible. It is said by some integrationists that the Bible deals only with "spiritual" matters. To illustrate this they draw a triangle with the words "Pastor, Physician and Psychologist" at the angles. The psychologist's thought is: "Let physicians handle bodily illnesses, let theologians and pastors deal with spiritual matters, and let us deal with psychological problems." Are these distinctions valid? We are thinking especially about the distinction between the "spiritual"

---

30   This is admitted by Carter and Narramore: "Both the Bible and psychology have a great deal of subject matter in common." Op. cit. p. 15. Collins says as much: "psychologists and theologians both study human behavior, values, interpersonal relations, attitudes, beliefs, pathology, marriage, the family, helping, and problem areas such as loneliness, discouragement, grief and anxiety. The two disciplines have similar interests and some overlapping goals." Gary Collins and H. Newton Malony, Psychology and Theology: Prospects for Integration. Abingdon: Nashville (1981), p. 13.

and the "psychological." And by the way, what is a "psychological problem" anyway?[31]

What is Spiritual?

Isn't helping counselees live lives filled with love, joy, and peace wholly a spiritual matter? Paul seemed to think so when he wrote "the Spirit's fruit is love, joy, peace, patience, kindness, goodness, faithfulness, meekness, self-control" (Galatians 6:22, 23)! Significantly, Paul says that these qualities are produced by the Spirit. If anything ever was a "spiritual matter," surely it is that which is the work of the Holy Spirit. The pieces of fruit listed in Galatians 6 are *His* "fruit" (i.e., the result of His work). How, then, can Christians who are psychologists claim that some psychological system can bring about the same results? The answer? By not talking about the problem; it is easier to sidestep it than to grapple with it.

Competition

I don't know how you'd describe it if two firms open stores on opposite corners of an intersection, each selling cars, but I'd call it competition. If psychologists open shop claiming they can produce the very same qualities that the Bible says the Spirit does, that too is competition. And, as the Old Testament so vividly demonstrates, God doesn't bless His competition. Can the two be reconciled? Only by denying the unique character of the Spirit's work! So, the distinction between truly Christian Counseling and psychology-as-done-by-a-Christian is valid.[32] The two are not alike, though

---

31 In almost every case when reading of "psychological problems," I find that dropping the word "psychological" and simply reading "problems" leaves the meaning unchanged!

32 But certainly not because one deals with spiritual problems and the other with psychological problems. Indeed, supposed "psychological problems" are in reality spiritual ones. The difference between Nouthetic (or biblical) counseling and psychological counseling is that one was ordained by God as the (continued on the next page)

they cover much of the same territory. The one is biblical; the other competes with it.

"Well," says someone, "Perhaps the Spirit works through psychology. If that is true, it would harmonize things, wouldn't it?" No it would not. The two views are so antithetical that to say that the Spirit might work cooperatively through the methods of a pagan, psychological system is near blasphemy. Listen to Bob Hoekstra: "Psychological counseling cannot contribute to sanctification. Sanctification is a work of God, by His Spirit, using His truth."[33] He explains this statement by pointing out the fact that psychological systems are but "human" systems of man's "wisdom aiming, in part, at increasing a person's ability to change his own life through his own human resources."[34] Hoekstra is right! Not every Christian who does counseling omits the Spirit and the Word, of course, but Hoekstra is correct in observing that the system being used – if not entirely biblical in nature – has this ungodly, self-sufficient "aim."[35] Self help change, even when assisted by a psychologist, cannot be blended with sanctification. They clash!

Methods Differ Radically

Moreover, as I have shown elsewhere, builders of systems will develop methods, if they are designed by tight thinkers, to achieve

---

    proper way to counsel, while the other was not. So while there is a valid difference between the two approaches, it is not that which is mentioned above. Rather, it is that one is the reality; the other is the ersatz.

33 Bob Hoekstra, *How to Counsel God's Way*. Living in Christ Ministries: Murreta. (1999) p. 42.

34 Ibid.

35 At every point, the goals of believing and unbelieving counselors will differ. Take, for instance when a counselee comes seeking relief from some problem. The psychologist, using unbiblical methods, will adopt those that aim at relief. On the other hand, a Christian counselor will aim at helping the counselee to do what pleases God – whether or not relief follows.

the aims of those systems. This means that if a Christian borrows methods from some non-Christian psychological system, he will be using methods aimed at something other than what God desires. Sanctification – if it is true biblical sanctification (and not some substitution for it) – can be produced only by use of biblical methods and means. To begin with, then, we must understand that, unlike the non-Christian psychologist, the Christian counselor "aims" to please God in the problem, no matter what it may be, and desires changes to that end. There is no correspondence between the aims of unbelievers' systems and the goal of true Christian counseling.

Genuine Sanctification

The biblical counselor, then, will use only those methods arising from and developed in accordance with the Scriptures since he knows that these methods alone can bring about godly change. The counseling of each of the two, therefore, will differ radically. Surely the changes described in Galatians 6, referred to above, are the work of God's Spirit as the counselor ministers the Scriptures; not those that some non-Christian counseling method was designed to achieve. False look-alike "sanctification" can be brought about by adopting and using methods foreign to Scripture, but only the Spirit at work in the believer through His Word can bring about the genuine change that pleases God. Paul put it this way: "Those who are in the flesh cannot please God" (Romans 8:8).[36] By "flesh," as the context shows, he meant those who do not have the Holy Spirit in their lives. What they do must be done purely by human (or "fleshly") means and methods. All change that at bottom is not the work of the Spirit displeases God.

So much for sanctification in general.[37] I put sanctification first in our present discussion because it ought to be the goal of

---

36 This verse, refers to unbelievers. Extend it: can unbelieving psychologists please God?
37 Sanctification is a "setting apart." It is the progressive work of laying aside old sinful ways while replacing (continued on the next page)

every Christian counselor to help his counselee become more like Christ as he puts off past sinful ways and replaces them with new biblical ones.[38] Biblical counseling aims at removing obstacles to sanctification which replacing these with biblical alternatives that encourage it. What is true of sanctification as a whole is also true of all the elements involved in bringing it about. Consequently, they too must be biblically-based and biblically-derived. Otherwise, they cannot achieve biblical ends.

Church Discipline

I have spoken of methods adopted by those who truly do biblical counseling, and in the footnote referred you to fuller discussions of the matter to which you may turn if you wish. But, for a concrete example of how those methods are quite distinct, consider the use of church discipline found in Matthew 18:15ff.[39] How can the non-Christian counselor adopt this as a method for change? Of course he doesn't want to and could not if he did; it is totally foreign to him. And he does not have the ways and means of disciplining his counselee even if he wanted to, since that can only be done within the framework of the Church. Yet, as Jesus says in that passage, whenever two or three are gathered together[40] to discipline an erring brother or sister, He promises to be in their midst. That means He works through this method of dealing with His people. If we want to bring about God's change (the change He says He desires), we must use God's methods – including church

---

them with their biblical alternatives. Thus it has a negative side and a positive side. In short, it is becoming more and more like Jesus Christ.

38 See my books *What About Nouthetic Counseling?* (p. 73) and *Joyfully Counseling People with New Hearts.*
39 I have mentioned church discipline because it so sharply divides Christian counseling methodology from that of others.
40 The context shows that this has nothing to do with small prayer meetings!

discipline which He designed specifically to bring contumacious counselees to repentance and restoration. So, if Jesus works through church discipline to change counselees, as He said He would, why would one adopt a psychological system that fails to include Him?[41]

The Spirit's Work

We must ask again, how does one obtain Truth? I have spoken quite fully about this matter in earlier chapters, but allow me to add a point. Thinking of methodology, we must remember that Jesus told His disciples that "when the Spirit of Truth comes, He will guide you into all truth" (John 16:13). How did the Spirit do this? Peter says, "men who were carried along by the Holy Spirit spoke from God" (II Peter 1:21). All the Truth necessary to establish and supply the church with whatever it needs for life and godliness (II Timothy 3:17; II Peter 1:3) is found in the Scriptures, the book that the Spirit moved its writers to pen. It is His book; a book in which He spoke in the Old Testament,[42] and in which Jesus says the apostles would further write inerrant Scripture as His chosen means to speak in their day (through the New Testament). Why, then, would anyone who believes the Bible refer loved ones and parishioners to those who (at best) try to blend men's ideas with the Word of God in counseling – even though they may be believers? Their faith may be genuine but, sadly, they use the theories and methods of unbelievers. In the next chapter, I shall continue to show how psychology and biblical counseling cover the same territory, but in quite different ways. If you have not already done so, I want you to think about something: have you determined on which corner you will buy your automobile – and from whom?

---

41 The extent to which church discipline has vanished from evangelical churches today in favor of every other way of dealing with sinning Christians is clear evidence of how much the world's methods have replaced biblical ones.

42 See also Hebrews 3:7, 10:15 where we are told that the biblical writers spoke the word of the Holy Spirit.

Chapter Eight

Conflicting "Revelations"?

General/Special Revelation

We have seen that the nature and scope of General Revelation and Special Revelation differ. That is important in attempting to assess the role each plays in the providence of God. They do not cover the same ground. What General Revelation teaches is also taught in the Bible in detail, far more precisely. But what is taught by General Revelation is not, beyond the few truths we have mentioned, the same as that taught by Special Revelation. The latter is far more extensive. The one is non-verbal; the other is verbal. What difference does that make? If someone refuses to listen to a door-to-door salesman by slamming the door in his face without an explanation, the salesman gets the idea that he is unwelcome. But he doesn't know why. Was it his demeanor? The time of day? What? In contrast, if, before doing so, a housewife shouts, "You're the fifth salesman to come today!" he knows a great deal more – specifically. The action and the word differ as General and Special Revelation do in the areas of overlap. But these areas are small in number since General Revelation is quite insufficient to meet man's problems (the very area of supreme importance to psychologists and biblical counselors, and precisely that over which Bible-believing counselors differ from each other).[43]

---

43 General revelation, however, ought to drive men to seek God.

Five Conflicting Views

But I promised to show that what psychologists call "God's truth" could not be such since it conflicts with the Bible. To state the case simply by the way of example,[44] I shall deal with five contemporary views that are propagated by Christians who do psychological counseling.

These are:

1. need psychology
2. self-esteem
3. alcoholism as disease
4. medication for non-organic problems
5. the importance of the past

Let's touch on each of these in order.

Need Psychology

Need psychology stems from Maslow's hierarchical pyramid of need. Each level of the pyramid rests upon the level beneath it. Before moving higher, the lower needs must be met. For instance, one must have experienced love of himself in order to love others. He simply cannot love unless he has known it. Hoekstra rightly says, "Need operates here as a disguise." He is speaking about how people justify their desires and make choices by calling them "needs."[45] People move from one Bible-believing church to another because, as they say, "My former congregation wasn't meeting my needs." They leave marriages with the same excuse: "He/She didn't fulfill my needs." The person who speaks this way has the idea that these institutions exist for his benefit. Actually, marriage, the church, and dozens of other institutions exist as ways for Christians to show love toward God and others – not to meet their self-

---
44 A far greater number of examples might be given.
45 Op. cit., p. 82.

declared, self-centered "needs." According to I Corinthians 7:3 and 4, in regard to sex within marriage, each partner has obligations toward the other to "fulfill." And one's body belongs to the other, not to himself! I shall not develop this matter further (if you wish to read about it in more detail, see my Christian Counselor's Manual, pp. 391, 392). Clearly, need psychology does not fit the biblical pattern.

One of the serious faults in need psychology is revealed by the terminology used. People no longer simply say "I need a pen to write a letter," etc. Rather, they express themselves this way: "I had/have a need to …" and then they list everything from wanting attention to having sex with a neighbor. Need theology is out of accord with Special Revelation which teaches that there are only two biological needs: "food and clothing" (I Timothy 6:8), and one non-biological one: "there is only one real need"[46] which was to sit at His feet and learn from Jesus (Luke 11:40, 42). In characterizing modern Christian psychology, Hoekstra concludes, "But I do not believe they have thought deeply enough about what a need really is."[47] Plainly, such thinking, if it is to yield Truth, must arise from study of the Scriptures and not from psychology!

Self-Esteem

The second matter, closely related to the first, is the supposed need for self-esteem. Since I have studied this matter and found it wanting biblically in an entire book, entitled *The Biblical View of Self-Esteem, Self-Love and Self-Image*, I see no profit in duplicating that material here. Let it be said, however, that this once widely-proclaimed viewpoint is already being downgraded as a failure, and therefore passé (although for a while very strongly advocated by the

---

[46] While there is a textual problem here, the true reading is probably as given above. Nevertheless, if the passage says "few" instead of "one," it still eliminates the numerous so-called "needs" of modern Need Psychology.

[47] Op. cit., p. 83.

world). Belatedly, the church (which trails after the world) is now vigorously propagating it.

Alcoholism – the Disease Model

The third view is the long-standing idea that drunkenness is a disease. Advocated by Alcoholics Anonymous, and the many who follow them, this disease model has been dominant in both worldly psychology and "Christian" psychology (which is also worldly!). The concept is diametrically opposed to the Bible, which teaches that "drunkenness" is sin (I Corinthians 6:10) that can be overcome (I Corinthians 6:11) through the work of the Spirit of God (Ephesians 5:18). AA propagates the view "once a drunk; always a drunk," and advises its members that they must remind themselves of this every day. This is contrary to the biblical teaching that drunkenness may be overcome once and for all. Being filled with (by) the Spirit, Who is able to dominate one instead of wine, is a concept entirely foreign to A.A. and even many so-called Christian Counselors. Because of their distrust in the Bible, they do not believe that what Paul says is true – that drunkards, homosexuals, and others are able to overcome their sinful lifestyles by the power of God and put these behind them once-for-all. But consider: Paul, himself, was a murderer before his conversion (Acts 9:1). Do you believe that after conversion every morning he had to get up and remind himself, "I am a murderer and I must watch myself today not to murder anyone?" The notion is silly. As he said in I Corinthians 6, not only drunkards and homosexuals are able to put off these lifestyles, but murderers as well!

Medication

The fourth area that is big today is the notion that medication can solve personal problems. Franklin E. Payne, MD, writes:

> America is being medicalized. More and more problems facing both individuals and society are being

"medicalized." That is, they are being given either a medical or psychological "diagnosis." And – far too many Christians are following the pattern. "So what?" you ask. Just this.... You see, if these problems are medical or "psychological," then the afflicted person needs a physician, not the Great Physician. ... The second major effect of the re-classification of sins into medical/psychological problems is the economic cost. ... The realities are these. Sins can never be healed on a physical basis.[48]

If someone is anxious, worried, or depressed, he is immediately medicated. But that only masks the true nature of what is wrong, and it takes away motivation to discover and deal with the real problem. Since Bob Smith, MD, has written extensively about this matter, I shall refer you to his important volume, The Christian Counselor's Medical Desk Reference.[49] As crucial as it is to send persons with genuine organic problems to a medical doctor (who may rightly prescribe medication such as insulin), it is every bit as important to be able to distinguish medical from non-medical difficulties, the latter being those which Christian counselors should help overcome by using the Bible. Smith's book is designed primarily to help the Christian distinguish between the two situations.

The Past

Lastly, taking trips into someone's past is still prevalent in one form or other among many so-called Christian counselors – even though its roots are strictly Freudian. People like Crabb and Allender are well-known for doing so. I shall not prolong this

---

48 F.E. Payne in the *Journal of Biblical Ethics in Medicine*. Vol. 5, No.4, 1991, pp. 67. 68.
49 Incidentally, volumes mentioned favorably in this book are available (or can be made available) from Timeless Texts, 8261 Hwy. 73, Stanley, NC 28164.

chapter by delving into the matter since I have considered it in my first book, *Competent to Counsel*, and in a number of others since. The issue is very well treated in a book by Gary Almy, MD, *How Christian is Christian Counseling?* The belief that the cure for present problems is to be found in the past is dominant today both in Freudian teaching of various sorts and also in the Recovery of Memories movement which has caused so many difficulties for fathers whose daughters have been coached by "therapists" into thinking they have molested them. Almy's book quite convincingly exposes the problem. Biblically, there is no reason to dig into a person's past. In Scripture, we find the apostles doing no such thing. The New Testament counselor deals with the present situation.

Many Systems, None Accepted

These and a hundred other theories are proposed by psychologists and adopted by Christians who do psychology. They do so even though they contradict biblical revelation. Then, they attempt the impossible – to integrate Truth and error! Collins says, "There is no such thing as a Christian theory of counseling.... The best known of systems is the nouthetic counseling of Adams, although this might more accurately be listed as a pastoral, rather than a professional approach."[50] How is it that after so much time, study, and theorizing, there is no accepted Christian system of counseling? What is remiss? Clearly, a major reason is that in the theories set forth by integrationists there is nothing uniquely Christian to offer. Otherwise, why struggle to integrate?

---

50 Op. cit., p. 51. It is interesting that he contrasts pastoral and professional. The fact is, biblically speaking, God's professional is the pastoral counselor!

Chapter Nine

Psychological Empiricism

The average integrationist thinks of himself as an empiricist,[51] and seems proud of it. He usually speaks of utilizing the empirical method for discovering and obtaining truth as valid even though the results go beyond Scripture.[52] Malony says that he "accepts" empiricism for obtaining "truth through controlled experiments." He continues: "We can and must draw from other nonbiblical sources if we want to understand human beings … and bring about maximum change through counseling."[53] It could not have been put more bluntly. It is as if he had said, "The Scriptures are certainly inadequate when it comes to understanding people."[54]

Sufficiency Denied

Every integrationist denies the sufficiency of the Bible for bringing about "maximum change." Otherwise, why integrate? Certainly Paul thought otherwise about the matter. In speaking of

---
51 The word comes from the Greek, empeiria, meaning "experience." The empirical method relies upon observation and experience.
52 John warns against this in II John 9.
53 Op. cit., p. 35.
54 One wonders, then, if biblical knowledge was totally inadequate prior to the use of empiricism. If true, the church would – for over 2000 years – have been greatly deprived. Moreover, John would have been wrong when He said about Jesus that He "knew what was in human beings" (John 2:25).

Psychological Empiricism

the changes in people that Scripture is capable of bringing about, he wrote that the Bible is "useful" to "make the man from God adequate, and to equip him fully for every good task" (II Timothy 3:16, 17). By those words, in three different ways, Paul made it plain that those who use the Scriptures alone are sufficiently equipped to change people so as to enable them to please God. Now those who seek to bring about change through the Scriptures alone either are or are not thoroughly equipped for the task.[55] The views of Paul and of Malony are antithetical – they cannot be integrated! Who will you believe – Malony or Paul? Obviously, you can't have it both ways.

Because integrationists always want to add to the Scriptures they contradict the Bible. By the label "integrationist" they do not confer a compliment upon themselves. As a matter of fact, in the light of what Paul wrote, the title is a little short of being an accusation. It is dependence upon the empirical method that has led to the confusion and error that dog the steps of every Christian who is a psychotherapist. Because integration is based upon the erroneous idea that by empirical study one may add to his ability to counsel, the instructed Christian avoids its so-called "findings."

Scientific Empiricism

Empiricism is the basis for science,[56] which has resulted in the many breakthroughs of modern medicine and many of the conveniences that we enjoy today. Scientists are to be applauded for their successful use of the empirical method. But what is good for the goose is not necessarily good for the gander.

Why? Because when a Christian seeks to discover Truth about man's problems through the empirical method he denies the

---

55 For details on this passage, see my book, *How to Help People Change*, which is a book-length exposition of II Timothy 3:15–17. In this book I show that Paul was setting forth a process of change that is complete.
56 Psychotherapists relish the name "scientific" applied to what they do.

sufficiency of the Bible and ends up sinning against God and his neighbor. Psychology (the attempt to change people apart from God's Truth) is a seriously flawed enterprise, as we have seen. This is because, contrary to what he believes, the integrationist cannot discover in nature what God has already provided in the Scriptures. Observation, experience, and experimentation will never elicit Truth about man.

When this wrongheaded use of empiricism takes over counseling as the method of searching for Truth, the resulting situation is confusion and error. Indeed, empirical integrationists have found themselves floundering about like those gullible persons whom Paul described as "always learning and never able to come to a full knowledge of the truth"[57] (II Timothy 3:7). Unlike science, psychotherapy claims discoveries that, when analyzed through the biblical lens, prove akin to the "irreligious chatter and contradictions of what is falsely labeled 'knowledge'" (I Timothy 6:20). Paul urges Timothy to "turn away" from such things.

Scriptural Superiority

The Bible doesn't tell us how to manufacture medicines, how to design and construct skyscrapers, or how to drive an automobile. But it does tell us everything necessary to solve problems in living so as to live in a godly manner to God's glory and the blessing of our neighbors (II Peter 1:3). And what it says is applicable in every age and culture. If the Bible is sufficient for this, as it claims, then every Christian counselor ought to be satisfied with what God has revealed in it. Why go looking elsewhere?

Actually, Malony thinks that the empirical method is superior to the Bible, if the latter is not studied empirically! He writes,

> Reading the Bible is an experiential activity not unlike the psychologist's research in the laboratory. Only if the

---

57 Note the wide differences between Collins and Malony in the same book!

Psychological Empiricism

evangelical psychologist approaches the Bible this way will he have an authority comparable to the authority the non-Christian psychologist derives from his careful observation and accumulated experience of the human scene.[58]

In other words, the student of the Bible must "experience" the Bible empirically by testing it and discarding that which is not accurate if he is to discover Truth. If by that Malony meant the Bible must be studied carefully, he would be correct. But he does not say that. What he does say is that by this empirical approach to Scripture (putting it in the laboratory to be tested by man!) "many of the theological perspectives that we earlier regarded as infallible" will be "put aside"[59] It is unfortunate that all too often this prediction has come true. Much of the good theology that has been derived from careful exegesis of the Scriptures has been "put aside" by empirically-oriented psychologists! This has happened to their own detriment and to the injury of the church.[60]

All of this is for the purpose of having God "speak with one voice," says Malony, as the "sacred/secular split is overcome."[61]

---

58 Ibid., p. 94.
59 Ibid. Think of it! Testing what God has said in the laboratory of "experience." Malony says "We can believe only what we experience" (Ibid.). In this procedure, man's experience becomes the measure of what is or is not Truth! This is serious error! No wonder many biblical teachings are laid aside in favor of non-Christian beliefs by Christians who are psychologists. As a matter of fact, we must believe before we experience God's Truth. Otherwise, we would never accept anything as true and decide to enter into it wholeheartedly! Addressing Thomas, an early empiricist, Jesus said, "Happy are those who believe without seeing" (John 20:29). It is not always true that "seeing is believing"; when it comes to knowing God's Truth about man "believing is seeing."
60 Again, see Gary Almy (op. cit.) for case studies demonstrating this fact.
61 Ibid.

Is All Truth God's Truth?

Doubtless, by using the empirical method, harmony can be achieved. But the voice that speaks will not be the voice of God! Harmony will come about only by bending the Scriptures to fit empirical data. Integrationists, it seems, want to be like the world, accepting its methods and applying these to the use of Scripture. Rather, one cannot help but think that empiricism is an attempt to achieve in Christianity a new imperialism! To Malony all I can say is "baloney!"

Chapter 10

So What?

So, all Truth is God's Truth – so what? What's the big deal about investigating this slogan and concluding after chapters of discussion that it's true? It's a truism. But there are some who seem not to understand its meaning or its implications. As a result, our concern up to this point has been to show that, when we properly interpret the slogan, those who use it most fail to use it as they should. In reality, they have made their supposed search for "God's Truth" a search for man's wisdom – in the process, often adding to or subtracting from God's Truth.

But they have covered their actions with the slogan. Under the banner of "All truth is God's truth," they have tossed all sorts of worldly thoughts and methods into Christian churches and institutions. That isn't right, and it has been our purpose to point it out to the unsuspecting. Looking at some Christian congregations, you see a great deal of concern about evangelism, but little or none about genuine Christian counseling. Certainly it is right to want to Christianize the world but, unfortunately, today there is as great a need to Christianize the church!

A Berean-Like Attitude

But all of that's negative – necessarily so, sadly. Error must be revealed to warn the naive and counter the misleaders. Yet there is a very positive side to the search for Truth which certainly ought to be mentioned. The Bereans, for instance, were not looking for error; they were concerned about Truth. "Daily" they searched the Scriptures "with great eagerness ...to see if these things were true" (Acts 17:11). They were alert to the possibility of falsehood, but if there was any Truth in what Paul taught, they wanted to learn of it. And the way in which they checked his teaching out was to compare it to the Old Testament Scriptures. As a result, many of them believed the gospel. That is because they kept the right balance between avoiding error and searching for God's Truth. In our day, however, many plunge headlong into error through a mindless acceptance of integration, supported only by the utterance of the slogan "All truth is God's Truth." The Bereans would hardly have fallen into this trap. But what about the positive side of the search for Truth?

Jesus said to those who had believed in him, "If you continue in My word you are really My disciples" (John 8:31). Note two facts right off the bat: (1) genuine disciples continue to the end; (2) the thing that gives evidence of this fact is that they "continue" in Christ's "Word." Once again, we are pointed to the Word rather than to discoveries in "nature."

But of equal importance is what happens when a genuine disciple continues in Christ's Word (i.e., he *continues* to believe, search, and follow it). He will come to "know the truth and the truth will *free*" him (John 8:31, 32). That is the point that every counselor who wants to be biblical must recognize: what "frees" counselees of their sin and its consequences is the Word of Christ. The sin in which one is entrenched, when he comes to Christ as Savior, is slavery. It is the biblical counselor's privilege (and responsibility) to help him replace that slavery to sin by the glorious freedom which Paul called slavery to God! The Word of Truth – at all points – is involved in that freeing process. That is why it is so important to keep the Truth from being adulterated by anything else that may be called Truth – but isn't. It is at this very point that harm to counselees comes into play. The present discussion is not merely academic; it has to do with what the counselor says to and how he works with his counselees. And as if that were not enough, an even more important matter is how the counselor represents God. If he represents even the *best* of man's "discoveries" to date as God's Truth, he has far exceeded his rightful authority. Those who minister God's Word are not authorized to do any such thing. And, furthermore, to call man's discoveries "God's revealed Truth" is a serious misrepresentation of the facts.

Most of the problems that counselees have are sin-caused (ultimately, of course, they are all the result of Adam's sin).[62] This sin is either theirs or the sin of others who have acted sinfully toward them or have created problems for them. In every case, the Word is what sets men free from the "slavery" that sin brings. Jesus went on to say, "Let Me assure you, everybody who commits sin is sin's slave" (v. 34). Freeing people from such slavery is what Nouthetic Counseling is all about. I Peter 1:18, properly translated, is a clear cut instance of the principle. Peter is concerned about the "behavior" of his readers (v. 17). He wants them to bear a good testimony among those with whom they live as "resident aliens." And in order to do so, Peter informs them that they need to know that this is possible because of what Christ has done.[63] What has He done? Peter says that He set them "free" from "the useless behavior patterns that were passed down" from their "forefathers." This, He said, was made possible by "Christ's valuable blood" shed for them.

---

62 There are certainly problems that counselees come to have solved which are not the result of sin: premarital counseling, guidance, and information in general are among them. Nevertheless, at some point, sin seems to rear its nasty head in most counseling encounters.

63 Whether because they were having problems living up to their new status, feared that they couldn't do so, or were making excuses that they were not able to do, is uncertain. But the fact applies to every one of those possibilities.

Is All Truth God's Truth?

"But wasn't Jesus talking to unbelievers?" Yes and no. In John 8:31, John reports that He was speaking to those who had professed faith. Later, as the chapter shows, those who did not profess faith also became involved. But both the statement in verse 32 ("the truth will free you"), to those who did believe, and that in verse 36 ("If the Son frees you, you will be free indeed"), to those who did not believe, are still true and applicable today. Anyone who believes and continues in His Word will find freedom from sin and its consequences. These are all-encompassing statements: what we call aphorisms. That means that they have a life of their own. Aphoristic statements are bigger than the immediate context in which they appear; like proverbs, they apply across the board to every applicable situation. So it is clear from Jesus' words that it is His Truth, found in His Word, that frees people.

An Example

Now, take a case in point. In Galatians 6:1ff., we are confronted with a church situation that often occurs. A brother is "caught" (prolambano, which means to take by surprise, overtake, overpower before one can escape, seize, catch, or capture). It would seem that in this context the idea of being caught, entangled, or captured is what the apostle had in mind. He is in slavery to sin, and since he is not extricating himself he needs the help of another to "restore" him. Here is what the passage says:

> Brothers, even if a person is caught in some trespass, you who have the Spirit should restore him in the spirit of meekness, watching out for yourself so that you won't be tempted too (Galatians 6:1).

How should a counselor restore this brother? Through the ministry of the Word, blessed by the Spirit. The word "restore" means to make useful once again by such renewal as to make that which is restored capable of functioning as it was designed to. It is to *mend* what is broken. The term is used by fishermen and physicians. If a person breaks an arm, it is no longer useful so long as it is in that condition. It hangs uselessly at his side. The physician comes along and "mends" the arm so as to make it function as it was designed to function. The fisherman cannot catch fish with a torn net. It lies in his boat useless. So he "mends" his net in order to make it useful once more. The brother or sister caught in some trespass also needs counseling assistance to mend his life. In a sense that is what counseling is: mending that which is broken or torn.

Mending Counselees

The counselee once functioned more or less helpfully in the church. When he became entangled in a trespass, he became "useless" to the body of which he is a part. So, in love, the Christian counselor (one who has the Spirit – no unbeliever may be called upon to do so) bears his brother's burden by becoming helpfully involved in the problem (v. 2). He does this in order to make it possible for him to "carry his own [share of] load"64 (v. 5). It would seem then, that Paul is writing about restoring one to his place in the church so that, becoming useful once again, he may carry his rightful share of the load.

Free to Serve

At any rate, this is what freeing a brother from the clutches of sin *will* do. It will set him free to become a blessing to others. After speaking of the life of uselessness he had prior to conversion (Romans 6:21), Paul continues: "But now, having been freed from sin, and having become God's slaves, you have the fruit of sanctification for yourselves, and its result is eternal life" (v. 22). In other words, the believer has been freed in order to bear fruit that is a blessing to himself as he serves God. Obviously, since we have been

---

64 The word phortion used here means a "load that one is expected to bear." It was used of the soldier's pack. Cleon Rogers, *Linguistic Key to the Greek New Testament*. Zondervan: Grand Rapids (1980), p. 519.

set free from our former master (sin) we are now free to serve our new Master (God). Freedom, then, is not merely something that brings blessings to the one who is freed (as undoubtedly it does); of greater import, it frees him to love and work for his new Master. As Paul put it elsewhere, in slightly different terms, "Indeed, we are His handiwork, created in Christ Jesus for good works that God prepared beforehand so that we might walk in them" (Ephesians 2:10). God's purpose is to make us useful in His kingdom.

It is the Truth – the Word of Christ, Who is the Truth – that sets one free for service. There is nothing about General Revelation freeing anyone. Indeed, those who depend upon what they think is General Revelation only become further enslaved by doing so. Freedom from sin's slavery, and the problems that follow in its wake, comes only from believing in Christ and following His Word.

Well, now, after all of this discussion am I still prepared to say that "All Truth is God's Truth"? Of course I am. I affirm the fact with renewed vigor! Anyone would be a fool to say otherwise. "OK, then, is that Truth available?" Certainly. If one seeks properly in the right place. "If that's true, where can I find it?" To reiterate: in the Bible alone. That, in effect, is the sum of it all, isn't it? What's your answer?

Joyfully Counseling People with New Hearts

Jay E. Adams

Contents

Introduction 175
Preface 177
"Have a Heart" 179
No Valentine View Will Do! 181
The Heart of the Matter 184
The Hidden Heart 186
A Heart Problem 190
The New Heart is New! 193
Heart Idols and Graven Images 198
The Battle Lines Drawn 202
Counseling the Upright In Heart 207
Counselor Expectations 210
Is This Perfectionism? 217
New Hearts/New Starts 221
Some Practical Suggestions 224
Heart-to-Heart Talk 228
What's In It for Your Counselees? 232
Knowledge of Sin 237
Obey From the Heart 240
Experiencing the Joy of Counseling 243
Conclusion 248

Introduction

"What we need is less head knowledge and more heart knowledge." Did you ever hear a preacher say that? Did you ever say it? Indeed, before I learned better, I used to say it myself. Well, we were wrong – very wrong – when we did so. We led those who were listening astray, unwittingly demonstrated how not to interpret Scripture, and missed the point of the text, all in the same breath. It is because people misunderstand the biblical concept of "heart," because it is an important concept, and because every counselor must be able to understand and utilize that concept in his counseling that I have decided to write this book.

The mistaken usage mentioned above (which I shall consider later) is not the only way in which the biblical concept of heart is misunderstood and misapplied. There are those who refer to Ezekiel who speaks of "idols of the heart" (14:3), and develop an entire construct of counseling around that isolated passage even though it was not intended to be used that way. This, too, needs exploration.

Some believe that they may look into the hearts of their counselees to discover what is wrong and correct it. But the effort is not only preposterous (for that matter, who even knows his own heart?), it is a vain attempt to assume God's prerogatives.

In addition, there seems to be little understanding of the "new heart" that God promised through Ezekiel (Ezekiel 36:26, 27) and upon which He told Jeremiah that He would write His laws

(Jeremiah 31:33). Frequently, believers are counseled as if there has been little or no change in their hearts. That is to say, a counselor may fail to take the Christian's "new heart" into consideration.

So for these and other weighty reasons, I offer this volume to help biblical counselors everywhere so that they may have a grasp of the true biblical idea of "heart," they may teach and counsel without distorting the Scriptures, and they will have confidence to deal with the hearts of their counselees as God would have them do so. As a by-product (you might even say "bonus"), they too may whole-heartedly experience the joys of biblical counseling.

Preface

Many counselors – even biblical ones – find counseling disheartening. They consider it an ordeal, a task they dread or even avoid. Indeed, there are preachers who know that they should care for the pastoral needs of the flock, but who "can't bear" to counsel them. They excuse their negligence by saying, "I guess I just don't have the gift." But if they have truly been called to the pastoral ministry, they do have the gift of counseling since it is a vital part of the ministry of the Word. The truth is that they may not have developed it fully (gifts do not come fully operative; we must work at counseling just as we do at preaching). They may have convinced themselves that it is better for all concerned to send sheep off for help to someone who is not their shepherd. But as you think about it, doesn't it occur to you that there is something terribly wrong with that?

Such neglect need not always stem from laziness; it may originate in a dislike or fear of becoming involved in the problems of other people. It is easy enough to pontificate from the pulpit, but it is another thing to get down to working face-to-face with husbands and wives who do hateful things to one another, young people involved in drugs, and members who fight and argue. They see counseling only as distasteful, difficult, and often discouraging work.

Of course, counseling can become all three of these things – and more – if we let it. But, actually, when understood and practiced biblically, it can become one of the most exciting, rewarding, and even joyful activities in which a Christian can engage!

"Joyful?" you ask. Yes, joyful. There is hardly anything else in which there is more blessing involved than in leading a straying sheep to green grass and still waters.

"I'm not so sure about that," you say.

OK, then, will you give me the opportunity to try to convince you? In this book, I have attempted to set forth biblical reasons for saying what I have. It all starts with understanding the Scriptural truth that Christians are people with new hearts. Have you thought about that fact? Do you understand the implications of it? Are you willing to consider what these are? My hope is that you will as you read this book, and that as a result you will enter into the inestimable joys of truly biblical counseling.

Chapter One

"Have a Heart"

That's what some may think when they begin to read this volume. "Should you make so much of the use – or, for that matter, wrong use – of the biblical word 'heart'? Why stir up controversy concerning a word? Let it rest. Have a heart!" Well, I wish it were that simple, that we could pass the matter off with little or no discussion. Certainly it would be far more pleasant to do so. That's true especially because some of those I shall challenge are to one extent or another friends and fellow biblical counselors. Obviously then, it isn't out of any ill will or animosity toward them that I intend to discuss the matter. On the contrary, the purpose of this book is to help them (and others) to become more effective in their use of the Scriptures in counseling. It is my hope, therefore, that they will receive what I write in the friendly, caring spirit in which I write it.

The matter is of no little significance. Rather, how one understands "heart" in the Bible may have a strong influence upon much of his counseling. Why is that? Because, in the Scriptures, the word "heart" is frequently used to refer to much that is very important – especially to counselors. Its scope reaches far and wide. Indeed, it is so vital a matter that the Hebrew *leb* and the Greek *Kardia* (both of which are translated "heart") considered together occur 641 times in 570 verses in the New International Version of the Bible! Any concept with that range of usage cannot be ignored; it must be understood. That is, in part, what called this book into existence.

So I hope that once you have read the entire volume and have had time to reflect upon what is said, you will agree with me that one's understanding of "heart" is pivotal; that it is worth having studied and considered it in relationship to counseling. As a matter of fact, I dare to hope further that you will want to talk to your friends about the issue and, when necessary, help them to come to a more biblical viewpoint than they may now have. I hope that you will not only propagate a correct view of heart, but will make every effort to stamp out erroneous views.

So, then, *having a heart* (as I understand it) means to give full weight to the issue before us rather than passing it off as one of those peripheral matters that really makes little difference. I hope you will see that it is precisely because I *do* have a heart for counselors as well as for their counselees that I have undertaken this discussion.

Chapter Two
No Valentine View Will Do!

When someone says, "What we need is more heart knowledge and less head knowledge," he is making a play on the word "heart" as we use it in *Western* society. What he really means is that we need less of an intellectual, academic approach and more of an emotional feeling-oriented one. He is contrasting emotion with thought. As much as his sentiment may be needed in a given context, he is very wrong in that use of the word "heart" when referring to it in the Bible. "How is that?" you ask. "Doesn't everyone know that the word refers to the emotional side of one's personality?" Ah! But does it?

Evidently, there are many English-speaking preachers and other Christians who think so.[1] Their use of the word to describe emotion and feeling is all but universal. The word is regularly

---

1 I have discovered that as early as 1738 John Wesley was using the disjunction between head and heart in a standardized way that shows his readers were already familiar with it. John Wesley, *The Journal of the Rev. John Wesley* Vol. I. J.M. Dent & Co.: New York: n.d., p. 119. Probably the concept goes back to the scholastics. But Wesley and his bands of itinerate preachers may have done much to spread it among English-speaking people. No less an expositor than Lloyd-Jones fell into this error. In *A Tree by a Stream* he speaks of some who "emphasize the head too much, some the heart, some the will." In Edmund Smith, *A Tree by a Stream*. Christian Focus: Fearn, Ross-shire. (1995), p. 170.

181

associated with cherry-cheeked cherubs, pink hearts and lace doilies! To say "I love you with all my heart" carries the connotation of an ocean of emotion. But, as I said, that use of the term is Western, not Eastern. And the Bible is an Eastern book.

Indeed, in the Bible, the intellect is never severed from the emotions as it is in our usage. In Hebrews 4, for instance, you read of "the desires and the thoughts of the heart" (Hebrews 4:12). And in Genesis 8:21 every "intent of man's heart" is said to have been "evil," thus bringing on the flood. Clearly, in those passages (which are representative of many others) the intellectual side is firmly linked with the emotional. Both are viewed as stemming from one and the same source, the heart. There is no biblical disjunction between the two. In I Kings 3:9 we read of "an understanding heart," in Psalm 19:14 of the "meditation of my heart," in Romans 10:10 of "believing" with the "heart" and in Hebrews 10:22 of a "true heart." We read also of the fool trying to talk himself into believing that God doesn't exist by saying "in his heart, 'There is no God'" (Psalm 14:1). So in these, as well as in any number of other passages, the word "heart" is used of intellectual and other non-emotional activities. Clearly then, those who think of emotion over against other aspects of human activity when they read the term "heart" in a Scripture passage, tend to pour into the passage Western content that simply isn't there. Their view of the biblical view of heart is contaminated by Western usage. This can be dangerous because in many passages where there is no surrounding context to define the usage of the word "heart," the passage may be improperly understood by reading Western, emotional ideas into it. When we come to Scripture, we should bring an empty bucket. Otherwise we are likely to dip from the well only that which we first poured into it.

Take, for example, Psalm 51:17 where David prays about a "broken and contrite heart." In this passage, repentance is not thought of as merely (or even primarily) emotional, as if it were akin to regret. Rather, as in the rest of the Bible, repentance is first a change of mind and then a change of direction, all of which may (or may not) be accompanied by a great deal of emotion. It is not enough for the sinner to be "sorry" for his sins. His proud heart must be "broken" (disabled) and "contrite" (literally "crushed") so that it may no longer oppose God and His truth. He must come to think about his sins what God thinks and do about them what God requires. Consider also the tenth verse of this same Psalm: "Create in me a clean heart, O God." Plainly, what is involved is more than a request for proper emotions. Emotional change may or may not accompany the cleansing at that time; but the cleansing from sin so as to have a "pure heart" that is proper in God's sight is more than some sort of emotional catharsis! It involves a heart that thinks and determines one's activities according to the Bible. So you can see, it is important to have a right understanding of the word heart. One must understand it as the writers of the Scriptures used it. Otherwise, there will be a tendency to read "emotion" or "feeling" into passages, thereby distorting what the writers had in mind.

When we are told, "Above all" you must "guard your heart because it is the source of your life" (Proverbs 4:23), we should understand the "heart" as something central to all that we do. Certainly that means that the writers of Scripture considered the heart to be much more important than emotions. Indeed, they regarded the heart as so vital that, as Proverbs indicates, it is somehow or other (we shall see how in the following chapter) the very "source" from which everything in life flows.[2] That, certainly, could not be said of the emotions as over against the rest of the person. So, let us see what the word does refer to – if not to feelings.

---

2 John Flavel wrote, "The attractiveness of a Christian's walk springs from what takes place in the heart." In Edmund Smith, op. cit., p. 48.

Chapter Three

The Heart of the Matter

We have seen that the Western view, in which the heart refers to the emotions as over against the head (which refers to the mind or intellect), is not an accurate description of the biblical, or Eastern, view. To what then *does* "heart" refer in the Scriptures? If the contrast "more heart knowledge and less head knowledge" is an unscriptural contrast, then with what – if anything – is the word "heart" contrasted in the Bible? Notice the following passages:

Quoting Isaiah, Jesus says, "This people honors Me with their lips, but their heart is far from Me" (Matthew 15:8).

In Romans 10:9 Paul writes, "…if you confess with your mouth, 'Jesus is Lord,' and believe in your heart that God raised Him from the dead you will be saved."

In I Samuel 16:7 we are told, "…man looks at the outward appearance, but the Lord looks at the heart."

And in I Peter 3:3–4, "outward things" are contrasted with "the hidden person of your heart."

In all of these contrasts, whether it be of lips and heart, of mouth and heart, of the outward appearance or of the outer finery and the heart, it is the outer person that is contrasted with the inner person.[3] "Heart" is clearly used in the Bible to refer to all that goes on inside, whether it is thinking, planning, determining to set out on a course of action, self-talk, or feelings. *Your heart, biblically speaking, is the inner you.*

No wonder, then, that Scripture exhorts you to guard it with all diligence; it is the "source" of your life (cf. Matthew 15:19, 20). All that you think, do, and say comes from the heart. Since this is true, it is crucial for the biblical counselor (of all persons) to understand God's teaching concerning the heart. It is the heart that determines, plans, and motivates his counselees. And it is this heart, therefore, that must be brought into conformity to the Word of God at all points. Since this is true, and because it is of the utmost importance for you to learn all that you can about the heart, you can be grateful that God has told us much about it in His Word. Indeed, He has given counselors all the information that they need, to know how to tackle the many problems associated with human hearts (II Timothy 3:17).

To understand, believe, and count on that fact ought to result in building up a strong confidence for the biblical counselor. To begin a counseling case knowing that you come fully prepared to deal with it, ought to remove much of the fear and anxiety that those without such assurance often have. The counselor who uses the Bible need not try to impress counselees with bravado or psychological jargon; he brings into counseling the Word of the living God Who made man's heart, and tells him how to relate to it. What could be more impressive than that?

---

3 See also Psalm 24:4 where both the inner person ("heart") and the outer person ("hands") must be clean and pure to ascend into the hill of the Lord and stand in His holy place. Cf. Psalm 73:13, 78:72; Lamentations 3:41.

Chapter Four

The Hidden Heart

If you think about it, you will recognize that a person's heart is hidden from others. There is no way that another may look into your heart. Indeed, it is very difficult for *you* to look into your own heart to know your own intents and motives, let alone to try to uncover these things in another. That fact is of the utmost importance to counselors.

In one place, the apostle John, while discussing the assurance of salvation (which he calls "convincing our hearts" before God), has this to say, "…in whatever our hearts condemn us, it is plain that God is greater than our hearts and knows all things" (I John 3:20). His point is that one must trust what God says, not what one's heart may erroneously report about itself. The former evaluation must take precedence over the latter one. Clearly, John entertained the possibility that one's subjective determination of the matter might be faulty. He may fail to evaluate his heart correctly through simple error or even by self-deception.

Judgments about hidden hearts can be dangerous. The apostle Paul, writing to the Corinthians said,

> To me it is of little consequence to be judged by you or by the judgment of any other human being; indeed, I don't even judge myself. Now I am not conscious of anything against myself, but that doesn't mean that I

am innocent. The One Who judges me is the Lord. So don't judge ahead of time, before the Lord comes, Who will bring to light the things that are now hidden in darkness and will make the purposes of hearts to appear.

I Corinthians 4:3–5

Here the apostle explains how difficult it is even to judge what his own heart is up to, and leaves it to the Lord. God is the judge – no one else. All of this leads us to the fact that in two of the verses listed in the previous chapter (I Samuel 16:7; I Peter 3:3, 4) we see that man has neither the capacity nor the prerogative to judge another's heart. Paul rhetorically asks, "Who knows the thoughts of a person except the spirit of the person in him?" (I Corinthians 2:11). It is on this point that we must take issue with those who presume to do what they cannot and should not attempt to do. No counselor may look into another's heart. Man looks on the "outward appearance, but the Lord looks on the heart." Judging hearts is God's business! The heart is styled the "hidden person" by Peter. It is not visible or knowable to another human being. A counselor cannot know the heart of his counselee.

When speaking of the heart with which a human being is born, God says, "The heart is deceitful above all things, and it is exceedingly corrupt" (Jeremiah 17:9). Pointedly, He asks, "Who can know it?" implying that it is not possible for man to do so. In the next verse God answers His own question, telling us that He can "try the heart." In other words, He is the only One for whom this is possible.[4] As we search further concerning this matter, we see that God is addressed in prayer as "the Heart-Knower" (Acts 1:24), once more referring this task to Him in contradistinction to men.[5] It is, therefore, necessary for every counselor to recognize that his place is to humbly affirm his own incapacity to judge his

---

4 In verse 10 God also says that He tries the "reins" which refers to the emotions.

5 Cf. Psalm 44:21; I Kings 8:39.

counselee's heart and leave the task to God. We must repeat with Solomon, "You alone know the human heart" (II Chronicles 6:20, HCSB).

But, then, what can he do? First, he can rejoice that he is not required to search the hearts of others. He is not called to that impossible task; what he must do, therefore, is feasible. Moreover, God is at work in each counselee, trying his heart.[6] That means that the counselor does not work alone. The counselor ministers the Word, but the Spirit brings heart conviction through it. The final result is not, therefore, dependent on the skill and power of the counselor. This fact is significant.

If the heart is of such great importance, if it is the motivating power of a person's life, if it must be guarded above all things, somehow or other the Christian counselor must be able to deal with hearts. Given the fact that he cannot read others' hearts, that he is not the one who brings conviction, his task is minimal. That, too, should be encouraging. But what is that task?

Here are some things that he can do. He can discuss the necessity of guarding the heart as the Scriptures tell us to, he can take up questions of motive and the like with counselees directing them to evaluate these in the light of the Word, and he can warn them that an acceptable outward appearance is not enough since God looks on the heart.[7] In other words, he can explain biblical teachings about the heart and urge upon counselees the importance of getting their hearts right before God. And he can show them from the Bible how to do so. Beyond that, he can do little else, and therefore, he need do little else. For him to attempt to read his counselee's heart is to step over the line into God's territory. He

---

6 Especially as the heart is considered the "conscience" as it is in the passage from I John quoted above.
7 Richard Baxter asked those with whom he worked, "Did you take care to see if your heart is truly a new heart, if your heart is holy?" In Edmund Smith, op. cit., p. 31.

must remain in his own venue; it is God – and God alone – Who is the Heart-Knower (Acts 1:24). He must remember God's teaching that man looks only on the outward appearance. As James put it,

> There is but One Who is Lawgiver and Judge – the One Who is able to save and destroy. But you, who are you to judge your neighbor?
>
> James 4:12

Counselors must always avoid attempting to do that which they cannot do.

Chapter Five

A Heart Problem

In Matthew 15:19 we read that Jesus said, "From the heart come evil thoughts, murders, adulteries, sexual sins, thefts, false testimonies, blasphemies." At the heart of man's problems is the heart of man. Now, it is absolutely certain, as we saw in Jeremiah 17:9 (and here again in the words of the Lord Jesus) that sin comes from the inner person – the heart. It is an inside job! Man sins because he is a sinner– not the other way around. The description of man as it is set forth in these two verses, and elsewhere, depicts him as he is from birth, apart from a second birth.[8] It does not describe him after he has been given a new heart:

> Moreover, I will give you a new heart and put a new spirit within you; and I will remove the heart of stone from your flesh and give you a heart of flesh.
> Ezekiel 36:26

This latter description fits only regenerate persons.

The "heart of stone," with which all (apart from Christ) are born, like a stone, is dead, cold, and resistant to the things of

---

[8] It is an error of major proportions to apply to regenerate persons verses having to do with the unregenerate. This unfortunate tendency of some, causes misunderstandings and difficulty in counseling. Some have extremely low expectations as a result.

A Heart Problem

God. In contrast, the regenerate[9] heart of flesh is living, warm, and receptive to the things of God. Paul describes the two hearts and their responses to God's Word in I Corinthians 2:9, 14:

> But as it is written: What the eye hasn't seen and the ear hasn't heard, and what hasn't been conceived by the human heart, is what God has prepared for those who love Him....But a natural person doesn't welcome the teachings of God's Spirit; they are foolishness to him, and he isn't able to know about them because they must be investigated spiritually. But the spiritual person is able to investigate everything while (on the other hand) nobody has the ability to investigate him.

The human heart in the natural person (one to whom nothing *super*natural has happened) resists the Spirit's teachings in the Scriptures. There must be a "new heart" present in order to bring about the changes in a counselee that please God. This new heart supplies ability to understand and to do what God requires.

The natural person's heart is so oriented that he can't even "conceive" of the things that God has prepared for those who have the new heart, which enables them to love Him (see I Corinthians 2 [above] and Romans 5:5). But He has revealed these "things" *in this life* to those who are His own (In I Corinthians 2:9 Paul was writing not of future benefits but of present ones.) These wonderful gifts of His grace can be known by the unregenerate only in outward, superficial ways (cf. Hebrews 6:4, 5), but never from the heart. Assuredly, then, there is a heart problem which must be cleared up before biblical counseling is possible.

---

9 The word "regeneration" is used in several ways. I am using it throughout this work to describe "quickening," the impartation of spiritual life (Ephesians 2:5) which enables one to understand and believe the Gospel and begin to live for Christ. Where there is regeneration, sanctification always follows.

The object true Christian counselors have in view is to help counselees to honor and please God by bringing about the changes in counselees that He requires. Christian counseling cannot be provided for the unregenerate since it is impossible for them to honor or please God. So wise counselors make this clear and evangelize rather than counsel unbelievers. Such counselors will not settle for outward change that does not flow from and correspond to an inward change of heart. Obviously, in all of this, the heart is central.

Chapter Six

The New Heart *is New!*

For many years I have had a problem with atrial fibrillation, a heart problem. From time to time this difficulty acts up, and I must go to the hospital for a cardioversion. This means that a shock is sent through the heart. When the procedure is successful, nerves that ought not to be firing are quieted and the one that should be firing takes over. Then, the pulse beats in rhythm once again. My friends joke about my heart having been "converted" more than once. However, when cardioverted, I don't get a new heart in the process. It remains a heart with an internal problem. Because of that, I may need more cardioversions in the future. That is the way some seem to think it is with the spiritually-converted heart.

But, in one important respect, that simply isn't so.[10] When God changes the heart, old things pass away and everything is brand new (II Corinthians 5:17). In spite of this fact, though Christians talk about heart conversion, it seems that for many, such language refers to an ideal, not a practical, concept. Counselor, do you really believe that your Christian counselee – with all of his problems –

---

10 In another respect you can find a clear parallel. In the new heart, the main nerve that fires is like the one that seeks to please God. The Holy Spirit sends the shock through the heart by His Word to silence the other nerves (sinful impulses) that cause problems for the Christian.

has a new heart with which you may work?[11] Whether or not you do makes all the difference in counseling.

Alexander Stewart of the Free Church of Scotland has this to say:

> The regenerating power of the Spirit of Christ creates a new heart within men, and on the fleshly tables of the heart, as distinct from the unresponsive tables of stone which represented the external authority of the Old Covenant, the law of God is written. The result is that the impulse to obedience comes from within. Under the constraints of love and gratitude the believing soul walks before God in newness of life.[12]

Not enough attention has been given to the new heart in the regenerate believer. But to the biblical writers it was nothing short of astounding! Paul, for instance, conceives of this change as so radical that he can refer to it as nothing less than a "new creation" (II Corinthians 5:17). He goes on to declare that "everything old has passed away" and that "brand new things have come into being." Peter tells us that we have become "partakers of a divine nature"[13] by which we have "escaped from the corruption that is in the world because of desire" (II Peter 1:4). John says, "Whoever has been born of God defeats the world" (I John 5:4). These remarkable statements ought not be easily brushed aside – as so often they have been. Rather, they (and a host of others like them) ought to be unpacked and contemplated to the full. If they mean anything, they mean that the Christian has new capabilities and a new orientation. They mean that it is truly possible for him to

---

11 Fundamentally, then, the problem Christian counselors confront is not a heart problem. The new heart is on their side!
12 Alexander Stewart, Jeremiah; the Man & his Work. Knox Press: Edinburgh, n.d., p. 207.
13 That is, a nature that is divinely-given. It does not mean that we have become divine!

please God by understanding, welcoming, and following His will here and now.

Because that is true, we may no longer speak of the regenerate person in terms of the passages that refer to his pre-regenerate condition. I have mentioned, for instance, Jeremiah 17:9, where the heart of the unregenerate is described as "deceitful" and "desperately wicked." That verse refers to apostate Jews, not to regenerate believers in Jesus Christ. Similarly, in Matthew 15:19 where a whole string of sins is said to come from the heart, Jesus is speaking of unbelieving hypocrites who rejected His message (see vv. 1–18). Surely, what we find in these verses is not what we would expect from God's new creation in Christ, is it?[14]

Contrast those verses with these statements by James P. Boyce: "The regenerate heart has new affections and desires and is, therefore, fitted to seek after God and holiness."[15] And again, "The heart is the soil in which the seed, the Word of God, is sown, and that seed only brings forth fruit in the good soil. The heart is made good by regeneration."[16] Here, he refers to the words of Jesus in the parable of the soils. It was there that Jesus said, "And those on good soil are those who, when they hear the Word, hold on to it with a fine and good heart and persevere until they produce fruit" (Luke 8:15).[17] Boyce goes on to speak of sanctification as "a growth from the seed planted in regeneration, which is constantly bringing forth

---

14 N.B., in Romans 7:18, Paul insists that "nothing good dwells in me, that is, in my flesh." He does not say, "in my heart." By "flesh," as we shall see in chapter eight, he means his body, wrongly habituated.
15 Abstract of Systematic Theology. The den Dulk Foundation: Escondido (1887 reprint), p. 379.
16 Ibid. pp. 380, 381.
17 The good soil which is described as a "worthy and good heart" is the heart prepared by God's sovereign regeneration to receive the seed (cf. Luke 8:15). Nor should Luke 6:45 be ignored: "A good person from the good treasure that is in his heart brings forth good things…a person's mouth speaks from the abundance of his heart."

new leaves, and new fruit."[18] These statements exactly set forth the facts as plainly presented in the Bible.

Even in the Old Testament, God could say, "Asa's heart was blameless all his days" (II Chronicles 15:17), Solomon's was "understanding, wise and discerning" (I Kings 3:9, 12), and God could refer to those whose hearts are "completely His" (II Chronicles 16:9).[19] These, not the other sorts of passages, ought to be applied to regenerate people. Cease using the wrong passages, if you have been doing so!

Well then, what may be expected of the regenerate? That question is rarely addressed by persons who repeatedly and unthinkingly refer the same passages to both the regenerate and the unregenerate. It is a matter that should not be ignored. Indeed, using proper Scripture to describe God's people ought to be central to every counselor's thinking. Therein lies his hope for change. If he can hope for nothing more than continued streams of sin pouring forth from new hearts, just as they did from old hearts, what is the use of counseling? How much change may he expect? With what is there to work for change? If regeneration did not bring about radical improvement in the condition of the believer's heart, then what did regeneration do for him? If the coming of the Spirit into His heart does not enable him to love God and neighbor (as Paul indicates in Romans 5:5 that it does), then the Scriptures misinform us. But the Bible does not lead us astray. Its message offers genuine hope to the counselor. His work need not be in vain. People with new hearts can change – appreciably![20] With Paul, every

---

18 Ibid. p. 414.
19 The words "blameless" and "completely" used in these verses and elsewhere are translations of shalam and tam, which mean "to be entire." This refers, as we say, to "having it all together" so as to be growing spiritually in every area of life. James fleshes out the concept in James 1:4 where he speaks of the telios ("complete") man.
20 Calvin goes so far as to say, "a believer contradicts himself when he turns to sin." In Edmund Smith, op. cit., p. 119.

Christian counselor may urge, "So then, as God's chosen people, holy and dear, put on compassion, kindness, humility, meekness and patience" (Colossians 3:12). If it were not possible to do so, then he wrote in vain, and we counsel in vain.

How is it that change like this may come about? According to Ephesians 1:16–18, the Spirit, Who is Christ within the believer's heart, powerfully strengthens him to make it possible for him to serve God as he could not in his unregenerate state. When Christ "dwells" in the Christian's heart, He helps him to become "rooted and grounded" in love (Ephesians 3:17). The picture that Paul paints in this passage is very different from that which is sketched in Jeremiah 17:9! Writing to Timothy, Paul can speak of this young pastor as pursuing "righteousness, faithfulness, love, peace with those who call on the Lord from a clean heart" (II Timothy 2:22). It is the difference between the regenerate and the unregenerate heart that he has in mind.

What, specifically, is the new heart like? How does the biblical counselor plug into this newness in his counseling? Those are questions with which we must be concerned. But first, there is another matter that we must consider.

Chapter Seven
Heart Idols and Graven Images

There is a growing tendency among some biblical counselors to look for idols in the heart of every counselee. To search for and identify these "idols" seems to be their goal and is considered to be the secret to successfully dealing with a counselee's problems. Just about every counselee is supposed to worship some idol that he has set up in his heart in the place of God. What must we say of this?

To begin with, we must ask where the idea comes from. The answer is Ezekiel 14, where Ezekiel speaks of the elders of Israel setting up idols in their hearts (vv. 3, 4, 7). Although this passage is used as support for the idea, actually, there is nothing in it that even suggests the view just mentioned. The people of God to whom Ezekiel preached had become estranged from Him by their idolatry: "their heart continually went after their idols" (v. 5). They had been worshipping images of the gods of the nations round about them. They refused to listen to God's prophets and, instead, followed the advice of false prophets. It was for this reason that God was exiling them to Babylon. By that punishment, at once He was giving the land her sabbaths (which had not been observed), and He was cleansing the people from idolatry. J. G. Aalders wrote:

> The period of exile taught the Jewish people a lesson. In Babylon they learned to reject idolatry. In the post-

exilic period the Jews displayed a thorough dislike for idols.[21]

Yet, even in the midst of judgment, this change did not come readily; the elders of Israel had not yet learned from or repented of their sinful attachment to the idols that they had left behind. So Ezekiel had to confront them about their continued idolatry. If they could no longer have their graven images present to bow down to, they would retain them in their hearts. What they could no longer have in their physical presence they would set up in their hearts and, in Babylon, go on worshipping them anyway. This was in utter defiance of God.

The references to idols of the heart is but a mere statement of fact condemning them for idolatry in their hearts even when the physical images they had previously worshipped were no longer available. They carried internal images of the gods of Canaan and the surrounding nations in their hearts (i.e, in their minds). Ezekiel's words were written to unregenerate leaders who had apostatized from the living God. We know this because God was "cutting them off" from His people (v. 8). Neither the statements relating to idols of the heart nor the context has anything to do either with counseling or with believers.[22]

---

21 In Philip Hughes, ed. *The Encyclopedia of Christianity*, Vol. 4. The National Foundation for Christian Education: Marshallton (1976), p. 144. Cf. Jeremiah 5:19; 44:2, 3.

22 The only passage that even comes anywhere close to this – although it is actually very far from the idea of looking for idols of the heart – is Colossians 3:5 where Paul says that "covetousness is idolatry." Here, in a list of sinful habits, Paul mentions the fact that one of these stems from an idolatrous attitude. Far from stating that the other sins in the passage are idols of the heart, he singles out but one as such. This makes sense since the one who covets, in contrast to his other sins, tends to idolize that which is coveted. Unrighteous anger (murder in the heart), for instance, involves no such idolatry.

Secondly, the phrase "idols of the heart" was not set forth as a construct for discovering and dealing with sin in counselees. Neither the context nor the wording in it lend any credence to such a view. Indeed, in this place alone does one find anything about idols in hearts. Throughout the rest of the Scriptures various sins are referred to as sins, not as idols. They are discovered and dealt with in ways other than by identifying them as particular idols of the heart. The concept was a one-time usage peculiar to the circumstances of the time, and was not intended to be applied to all sorts of other situations.

There is a danger in creating a construct to apply to individuals in counseling when there is no biblical reason to do so. It is always dangerous to misuse the Bible by making passages do duty that they were not intended to do. There also is danger in elaborating on that construct to seek out specific "idols" such as "idols of lust, of wealth, of fame" and the like. Again, the context lends no support to any such thing. In time, this supposed approach could develop into a system akin to that which seeks to identify and cast out "demons of lust, fame," etc., with some of the attendant evils that are connected with it. While not all who use this approach are guilty of such things, there is a good possibility of drift in that direction.

In addition, it should be noted that Ezekiel was not told to probe for whether the elders had idols in their hearts, or to try to determine what, specifically, these idols were. No. The variety of their idols is not even in view; it is the fact of idolatry in the heart that is central. Note: Ezekiel merely informs the reader about what God has seen and revealed to him. It is He, the Heart-Knower, who has detected the idols in their hearts – not Ezekiel. Again, as we said in a previous place, there is no warrant for counselors to judge their counselee's hearts.

Indeed, we shall see presently, in contrast to some idol-locating system for dealing with the hearts of believers, what the apostles did use as a construct for helping Christians change. They are not silent on the matter, as they are about "idols of the heart" to which, incidentally, they never so much as allude.

Chapter Eight

The Battle Lines Drawn

When fighting sin in the life of a believer, if the strategy should not be centered on locating and eradicating idols of the heart, what should it be centered on? That is the important question. Put another way, if the apostles did not write about dealing with idols of the heart, about what did they write? What was the counseling construct that they used?

There should be no doubt about the matter in the minds of Christian counselors: to be biblical they must understand and fall in line with Paul and the rest of the New Testament writers who address the subject. We must be sure to draw the lines of battle where our great Commander-in-Chief has told us to, not in some other place. Otherwise, we not only fail to heed His words, but we may also fail to win the battle.

In the sixth, seventh and eighth chapters of the book of Romans, Paul has addressed the problem of sin in the believer in the fullest way possible. As he describes the enemy for us, he says nothing about uncovering and removing idols from the heart; rather, the enemy he identifies is sin in the members (cf. 6:12, 13, 19; 7:23). In addition, other terms that he uses as equivalent to that expression are "sin dwelling in me" and sin "in my flesh." In these vital chapters, Paul speaks clearly of the problem as sin dwelling in his flesh (i.e., in his "body") and in his [bodily or fleshly] "members." The problem was not difficulty with idols

The Battle Lines Drawn

of the heart, but in some way he had a problem with his fleshly or bodily members.[23] As a matter of fact, in Romans 6:6, Paul refers to his body as "sinful." (Not in a Gnostic sense. His meaning is that the body has become habituated to sin.) In Romans 7:24, he calls it a "body of death."

Now, note what he says of the believer's "inner person" (or heart) in Romans 7:22. Jeremiah predicted that the law would be written in the Christian's inner person, on his heart (Jeremiah 31:33). It seems that when Paul writes, "I delight in God's law in my inner person" (Romans 7:22), he is referring to Jeremiah's prophecy. And he goes on to say, "I see a different law in my bodily members fighting against the law of my mind and holding me captive to sin's law that is in my members" (v. 23). This "different law" (v. 23) is different from "God's law" mentioned in verse 22, which he indicates is the same as the law of his mind. So, in one way or another, Paul is saying that sin's continued sway over his bodily members often keeps him from doing the things that he really wants to do. What he wants to do (in his heart) he doesn't always do in his life because – in some way – the body gets in the way!

What is Paul talking about? Well, Paul was no Gnostic who believed that matter is inherently evil. He did not consider the body, per se, sinful. But, in the Fall, something began to happen to the body that regeneration does not automatically erase. What is that? It is what has happened to its "members." Each person is born with a corrupt heart that from his earliest days (Psalm 51:5; 58:3)

---

23 Every indication is that Paul is speaking of his fleshly body. He speaks of its "members" and equates it with "body." I take these expressions as referring to nothing less than the body itself. Without warrant, some attempt to make "flesh" and "body" in the text stand for something else (they have a harder time with the word "members" which, therefore, is often ignored). John Owen, for instance, speaks of body and flesh here as "figurative," the NIV translates sarx ("the flesh") as "sinful nature." And so it goes.

leads him into sin. He yields (or presents) his bodily members to sin, his master, as a willing slave (Romans 6:16, 19). They become habituated to the sinful patterns that develop. This is implied in the words "you presented your members as slaves to uncleanness and lawlessness to bring about more lawlessness" (Romans 6:19). As the members were used for sinful purposes they became habituated to these, which became patterns that automatically led to "more lawlessness." The patterns, once established, emerged whenever similar circumstances occurred. Thus, Paul is referring to his body as wrongly habituated.[24] That is to say, a body with its "members" habituated to act in sinful ways. These members of the body include the brain, which controls these habitual practices.[25] So because habits lead to unconscious, unpremeditated, skillful, and comfortable responses, sinful thoughts, attitudes, words, and actions soon become the norm.

But then, when Paul was regenerated by the Spirit Who gave him a new heart that was disposed toward God rather than toward sin, a radical change took place. His inner disposition and orientation began to look away from self and toward God. Paul now agreed with God's Word [law] in his inner person and from his heart wanted to follow it. But as Paul attempted to do so, he says that he found that "What I want to do I don't practice, but instead what I hate is exactly what I do" (Romans 7:15). He recognized a force in his members that hindered him from realizing many of his new goals in life. He found the old patterns taking over, and – before he realized it – he had sinned again! Paul says, "It is no longer I who produce it, but the sin that is dwelling in me" (v. 17).

---

24 Thus, the "different law" is the law of bodily habituation.
25 The brain's work is an aspect of the functioning of the "heart." This aspect of the inner person may become habituated. In II Peter 2:14, we read of those whose hearts are "trained in greed." The training of one's bodily members, through the training (habituating) of the heart which controls them, is carried over into the new life and must be dealt with.

By that statement, he was not shedding responsibility or making excuses; rather, he was uttering something of the frustration of the situation. Within one person two conflicting powers were at work.

Stewart speaks of "the tyranny of habit." He says, "Our actions have a tendency to reproduce themselves, and through repetition, to weave themselves into the textile of our character." Commenting on Jeremiah 13:23, he remarks that "It is a fatally easy thing to become 'accustomed to do evil.'" Even "vicious practices," he points out, "become easy and natural."[26] He says, "The Gospel of Psychology is poor comfort for a man who is struggling in the toils of his corruptions and lusts.... But Jeremiah has a message of hope." What is it? His "doctrine of the New Covenant with its 'better promises.'"[27]

Stewart rejoices over this:

> The reign of death is over, and the tyranny of habit is ended. For, on the new heart which He bestows, God writes His own law, and that means a new inward disposition "to do good," a new hunger and thirst after righteousness, and a new impulse to render obedience to the good and perfect will of God.[28]

In all of this, because of his new heart, the believer has the right approach, but must learn to marshal all his divinely-given resources to make the changes that will bring about victory. That, to a large extent, is what the biblical counselor helps him to do.

---

26 Op. cit, pp. 178, 179.
27 Ibid, p. 181.
28 Ibid. But, he goes on to observe, "When this radical change has been effected, however, it must not be forgotten that habit still has an important part to play in the life of men. It is possible to become accustomed to do good as well as to do evil, and good habits become a powerful ally of the Christian soul." The habit capacity, with which God endowed man, can be a blessing or a curse depending upon what it is he habituates.

Now, in his "inner person" the Christian "agrees with God's law" (v. 22), but he finds, as Paul put it, that his bodily members are "fighting against the law of my mind and holding me captive to the law of sin that is in my members" (v. 23). That, according to the Apostle, is the battle. It is not a battle to be fought with idols of the heart, but with sin in the members. When counselors point to some supposed idol of the heart, they distract the counselee, causing him to take his focus from the real enemy, thereby possibly leading to losing important battles with sin. Rather, the war must be fought in a way that will bring these members into conformity with the law of God:

> In the same way that you presented your members as slaves to uncleanness and lawlessness to bring about more lawlessness, now you must present your members as slaves of righteousness to bring about sanctification.
> Romans 6:19

In other words, there must be a rehabituation of the members of the body led by the new, regenerate heart. This can be done because Jesus freed us from sin's slavery (Romans 6:6) so that we could serve God. He is the One Who, by His Spirit, makes this possible. That is what Romans 8 teaches. So the dynamic to be learned must involve putting off the habitual, sinful ways in which from birth we trained ourselves to live apart from Christ, while at the same time replacing these with their biblical alternatives. For greater detail about how to do this see *The Christian Counselor's Manual* and *Winning the War Within*.

Chapter Nine

Counseling the Upright In Heart

In Psalm 64:10, David wrote, "The righteous shall be glad in Yahweh and shall take refuge in Him; all the upright in heart shall glory" (my own translation). According to this verse, there are people who are upright in heart.[29] The way that some (even Calvinists) write, you'd think it impossible to characterize anyone that way! The use of the word "upright" is a far cry from Jeremiah 17:9 where others' hearts are called "deceitful and desperately wicked." In Scripture, regenerate persons are described and treated differently from those who are not. They ought, therefore, to be considered different and treated differently by counselors.

The "upright in heart" are characterized as "saints" (set apart ones) and are spoken of as "dead to sin," "freed from the authority of sin," and "slaves of righteousness." Passages that are applied to unregenerate persons, therefore, ought not be applied to the regenerate as so often they erroneously are. Indeed, when Christians are addressed, the writers of the Scriptures characterize them as persons who are not only capable of serving and honoring

---

29 "Upright" in this Psalm comes from a word meaning "straight, even, level." The upright person is "straight" in God's sight. Today, we often use the term "straight" in a similar sense. (See also Psalm 15:2; 32:11; 36:10; 97:11; Jeremiah 24:7; 32:39; Ezekiel 11:19; 18:31, etc.)

God, but also as those with new hearts that want to do so. We saw in the previous chapter that Paul wanted to serve and please God.

The point, then, is that Christian counselors ought to talk to believing counselees assuming and indicating that they are fully capable of doing God's will and therefore will follow God's will because they have the resources to do so. This approach is very different from that in which the counselor thinks, "Well, perhaps my counselee may make some progress in sanctification in this life, but I don't expect very much." Instead, the biblical counselor is optimistic about what God has done in recreating the believer and giving him a new heart and His Spirit to fight the flesh. In no way is this an unrealistic view of the regenerate Christian. While it is only at glorification that one becomes perfectly holy, nevertheless, that is no reason to expect only meagre changes in this life. Instead, we must affirm that one actually can put off old sinful ways and replace them with new righteous ones. He is not forever stuck in his past. Some Christian counselors seem to act and think otherwise.

Too many Christians have a very low view of what God has done and will do for His people. They expect them to be fighting battles with the same sins for the rest of their lives. While there may be some who do so, that is certainly not inevitable. The apostle Paul, who was a murderer, could not rightly be called that after his conversion. The astounding change in vacillating, fearful Peter is another case in point. Over the years, we have seen counselees also make remarkable, lasting changes. Drunks no longer get drunk; adulterers no longer commit adultery. Indeed, opposite courses of thinking and acting replace old ones (see I Corinthians 6:9–11).

What I am saying is that a counselor rarely achieves more than he aims at. If his aim is low, the results will be low; if high, then the results will be higher.[30] His entire attitude, how he

---

30 Of course, the Lord graciously can do more for a counselee than we anticipate.

approaches counselees and the sorts of objectives he sets forth will all be affected by his view of the capacity believers have for doing God's will. If those who expect little receive what they expect – or less – they should aim higher.

In addressing the believing reader, Paul treats him as a new creature and shows him that the sin that he dragged into his new life from the past in the form of habit patterns is inconsistent with what he now may become in Christ. How one looks at himself is important. Unless he counts himself "dead to sin, but living for God in Christ Jesus" (Romans 6:11) he will hardly make much progress in putting off the old person and putting on the new person that he has become in Christ. It is time, then, that we as counselors recognize these facts and counsel accordingly. Addressing counselees as the New Testament writers did is essential.

This important fact does not mean that counselors should treat rebellious, sinning Christians as if it didn't matter. Exactly not that! It means that, the way they reprove them is crucial. Neither should counselors excuse them on the basis that little change could be expected; rather, they should confront them as failing to live up to the great potential that they have for serving God. The faithful counselor always enthusiastically holds out the prospect of pleasing God that now exists: "As a result [of parting ways with sin], it is now possible to live the remainder of your time in the flesh no longer following human desires, but following the will of God" (I Peter 4:2). That's how Peter confronted believers! Since what he wrote is true, counselors should cheerfully emphasize the fact! Let your counselees know that because God expects significant change in their lives, you do too.

Chapter Ten
Counselor Expectations

In the last chapter, we began to discuss the fact that the counselor's view of the regenerate heart in a believer ought to radically affect the approach that he takes toward his counselees. To lump believers together with the assorted counselees that darken the door of the unbelieving counselor down the street is a gross error. Yet, many counselors make little or no difference between them. No wonder there is little joy in such counseling. If there is nothing much for us to look forward to we should all be glum. But the biblical counselor has a very special clientele. So far as he is able to discern, he will counsel only regenerate people. Those who have a new heart, with its new dispositions, in whose heart Christ dwells in the Person of the Holy Spirit, and who are able to understand and appropriate biblical truth, are very different persons from those who receive counsel down the street. The upshot of this difference is that a Christian counselor who selectively counsels only Christians, may expect better results than others who do not.

Not only is this so, but he knows even before he begins that every true Christian he counsels has the potential for radical change. All of them can make changes that please God because of the fundamental change of heart that has already occurred. In addition, because they have the unparalleled resource of the Scriptures, and because they possess the power of the Spirit within, the biblical counselor looks forward with anticipation to what the Lord will do. That resource mix is the ideal combination for change. Why, then, should biblical counselors hesitate to counsel even in the most difficult cases? The reason cannot be found in some inadequacy of provisions – exactly not that! God tells those who serve Him in the ministry of His Word that He has provided all that they need to perform "every good task" which He calls them to undertake (II Timothy 3:17).[31] If inadequacy exists anywhere in the equation, it lies solely with the counselor himself. That is why it is essential for the counselor to come to a full realization of the potential that resides in the regenerate counselee, and to help the latter to do so as well. Only then will all "reasons" for failing to take on difficult counseling cases be exposed for what they are – nothing but pale, insipid excuses.

It is high time for elders in the churches, as well as other laymen, to take up the challenge of counseling. There is a great need for restoring the many believers who fail to carry their share of the load because they have become entangled in some problems which have come to occupy most of their lives and sap their energies (cf. Galatians 6:1ff). The elders are called to counsel formally as a part of the task of caring for the flock (see Shepherding God's Flock). Others, as a part of their mutual ministry to those who are members of the same body of believers, are also called to counsel "one another" informally (cf. Colossians 3:16; also see Ready to Restore, which is a book on counseling for laymen). Given the situation as described in the Scriptures, then, there is no reason for the church not to take on every counseling case that occurs among the people of God. No Christian should find it necessary to turn elsewhere for help.[32] Churches do not need to start counseling

---

31 For details, see my book, How to Help People Change.
32 John Newton wrote, "The Scriptures make plain all the principles and the working of the human heart, in all possible circumstances, and all the ways by which the heart is affected by Satan, by sin, by things of the world, by grace, by solitude or company in prosperity or affliction." In Edmund Smith, op. cit., p. 153.

centers; by its calling and definition every church is a counseling center!

The church should not only take on every case, but should do so with confidence and zest. Given the resources, the nature of the believer's new heart, and the presence and power of the Spirit, instead of hesitating, there should be wide-ranging and enthusiastic efforts by church members to help one another going on all of the time. After all, God not only calls us to such work but, from time to time, we all desperately need it. And He has provided all things necessary to assure success. There should be genuine pleasure among those who help one another when a problem occurs.

Moreover, the fact is that counseling provides one activity in which to see God at work up close and personally! Preaching sometimes has dramatic effects, but its results are often imperceptible as it gradually builds Christians up in their faith over periods of time. In counseling, as a marriage is saved, a young person is rescued from drugs, and lives are turned around in a multitude of ways, more immediate effects of God at work through His Word become apparent. Congregations which fail to experience these salutary results of the ministry of the Word in counseling often lack the kind of joy, enthusiasm, and reality that faith, rightly practiced, always produces. If your Christianity is stilted, wooden, and formalized, and in effect lacks reality, perhaps undertaking a vital counseling ministry is precisely what it needs. So, in wondering about how a counselor (or erstwhile counselor) should view the work of counseling in the local church (and it is work!), the answer is – he should enter into the task with joy, hope and alacrity. The fact, however, is that in many places there is hesitancy, fear, or downright failure to counsel.

Of course, counselors must have knowledge and wisdom as well as good intentions. Foolhardily rushing into something is not God's way. He speaks of one who is ready to counsel as "*filled* with all knowledge" and "*competent* to counsel" as well as "*full* of goodness"

(Romans 15:14). He is to counsel "with *all [sorts of]* wisdom" as Christ's Word "dwells *richly*" within (Colossians 3:16). To say, "I don't have those qualities" as an *excuse* for not counseling, is improper. All Christians are obligated to acquire them. The answer to a counselor's (or would-be counselor's) problem of the lack of resources is to quickly and earnestly work at their acquisition.

So, it is clear that Christians have an obligation to counsel, those who need counseling are capable of change, and God has provided everything necessary to make all the needed changes. Those are the amazing and heartening facts that add up to one thing – the church can and should counsel its own. And it should do so enthusiastically – joyfully expectant to see what the Lord will do.

Consider the advantage that the Christian counselor has over all others. Paul says that because of the change that Christ brought about, he "delights in God's law" in his "inner person" (i.e., in his heart), and that his "mind" fights against the ["different"] law in his "bodily members" (Romans 7:22, 23). So, when the counselor is working with someone like that, he may assume that his counselee's inner disposition is in sync with what he is trying to do. Paul further says that he is "serving God's law as a slave" with his "mind" even though, "on the other hand," he is "serving sin's law" with his "flesh" – his sinfully-habituated body (v. 25).

So, because there are new tendencies and a new orientation in the regenerate person, there is much to which the Christian counselor may appeal. When working with genuine Christians he should receive a sympathetic (even if sometimes frustrated) response:

> "John, I know that as a believer you must want to overcome your temptation to lust after other women."
>
> "You can say that again. Sometimes I agonize over the problem. Yet, I still can't seem to overcome it. Every

time I make a genuine effort I find myself falling prey to my old sinful ways. It's discouraging."

"Well, you are not alone. While it is certainly no excuse, your problem is understandable. The apostle Paul, himself, speaks about a similar frustration in overcoming sin in his life when he writes in Romans 7:14–15…"

"Yeah, that's how it is. Did Paul find an answer to his problem?"

"He did. And so can you. He says that the 'Spirit of life' dwelling within him 'freed' him from 'sin's law and death.' (Romans 8:2), enabling him to 'walk according to the Spirit' and set his mind on 'spiritual things' (Romans 8:5)."

"How did he pull it off?"

"He allowed himself to be 'led by God's Spirit' (Romans 8:14) rather than by the fleshly habits of his body. This 'leading' has nothing to do with guidance; it is leading in the path of obedience to the Scriptures – the Book that the Spirit inspired and which He uses to change people. In this way, like Paul, you can 'put to death your bodily practices' (v. 13), and your body can be rehabituated to serve God."

"Good. Let's get to work."

"Great. Turn to Job 31:1, 9–12 where the Spirit recorded some wisdom about your problem…" and so it goes.

You can see that there is a basic, inner sympathy in the regenerate counselee for serving God to which a counselor may appeal.³³ Sometimes that desire to please God must be dug out when it has been covered with layers of failure accumulated over a long period of time. It is wrong to think that the counselee will always want to resist; if his faith is genuine, more often than not, he wants to change. He may be discouraged over past failure. He may fear change. But you can always appeal to that fundamental desire to please God. What causes resistance is some complicating problem such as doubt or fear or the prospect of having expectations once again dashed through failure.

Referring to the Spirit's Book, in which He so realistically portrays the greatest saints as struggling with and overcoming sin, you can show your counselee how he too (through similar struggling) can do the same. This helps. Paul says that he was "shown mercy" so that he would become a "pattern for those who are to believe" (I Timothy 1:16). The counselor should recognize this and use Paul's example to help counselees who are struggling as he did. If Paul, who was a murderer, could find grace to put his "former manner of life" behind him, so too can your counselee. Encourage him by pointing this out and reminding him of the later life of the Apostle. So, take advantage of your advantages! Counseling isn't easy; change may come hard at times. But at length it will come – as it did for the Apostle to the Gentiles.

Your concern is to bring your counselee to the point where he expectantly prays with the Psalmist such things as "Incline my heart to Your testimonies" (Psalm 119:36), "May my heart be blameless in Your statutes, so that I will not be ashamed" (Psalm

---

33 Matthew Henry may be a bit sanguine when he writes about this matter, but his words point in the right direction: "And this new nature is given to all the saints, which puts a new life and vigor into them, strengthens them 'with all might in the inner man' (Col. 1:11) unto diligence in doing-work, patience in suffering-work and perseverance in both; and so all is made pleasant." Matthew Henry *The Pleasantness of a Religious Life*. Christian Focus: Fearn, Ross-shire. (1998), pp.116, 117.

119: 80), and where, in response, it could be honestly said of him that "His heart is steadfast, trusting in the LORD" (Psalm 112:7). When those things are true of him, it may then also be said, "His heart is upheld, he will not fear" (Psalm 112:8). Indeed, it will be true of him that he "doesn't doubt in his heart, but" because he "believes that what he is saying will happen, he will have it" (Mark 11:23). There is no reason to "lose heart" when you read of the promises of God to those who seek Him with their whole hearts.[34]

---

34 That is, not half-heartedly but genuinely, sincerely, and without doubts or hidden agendas.

Chapter Eleven

Is This Perfectionism?

"The way in which you are speaking about the new heart sounds dangerously close to Wesleyan perfectionism." No! No! A thousand times, No! I want nothing to do with that. It is only when we are finally with the Lord in eternity that the spirits of justified men are made "perfect" (Hebrews 12:23). That cannot happen in this life.

"Well, then, is this new heart of which you speak, perfect or not?" That is a good question. The Bible plainly speaks of the new heart upon which the Law of God is written, and declares that this new heart is capable of that which the old unconverted heart was not, but there is no place in which it is declared to be perfect.[35] Sin still comes from the inner person. Man's self (heart) is complex. It consists of all that transpires within a person – things that are good and those that are bad. As we have seen, much of the old life yet remains in the regenerate person in the form of habits of mind and action.[36] That is why Paul exhorts us to "put off the old person" that we were.

---

35 There are passages in which the King James Version translates words designating completeness as "perfection." This translation is misleading and must not be followed.

36 John Owen has this to say: "Every lust is a depraved habit or disposition, continually inclining the heart to evil." And he goes on to say that in "mortification of sin" (continued on the next page)

Some of that which is to be eliminated and replaced has to do with erroneous thinking. Some has to do with attitudes. And much is in the form of habitual actions. Habit doesn't have to do only with outward actions. It also extends to those inner habits of mind, attitude, and thought that remain, as well as those habits that have been newly acquired. These inner habits, of course, eventually lead to outward words and actions. Peter, for instance, speaks of "hearts trained in greed" (II Peter 2:14). That phrase has to do with the way in which one reacts as a result of his inner habituated values and thought processes.

Moreover, the new heart is far from realizing its full potential. There is much for it to learn – many of the old ways to overcome and a great amount of truth to learn and assimilate. The new capacity for understanding and appropriating truth from God's Word that comes with the new heart is vital. But it does not function in such a way that these things may be acquired automatically or instantaneously. Rather, one's "faculties" must be "*trained by practice* to distinguish good from evil" (Hebrews 5:14 [emphasis mine]). Practice in doing what? In understanding and following "the righteous Word" (Hebrews 5:13). And, as in the case of those Christians to whom Hebrews was written, having learned, one may even lose much of that learning and *become* "dull in hearing." Retrogression as well as progress, then, is possible. Two steps forward, one step backward is the way that things often go. So, the new heart has much to do to grow – and the growth that transpires within a person often comes in spurts. It is rarely even.

Nevertheless, that should not in the least detract from the fact that real, decided progress in things spiritual should be expected and may actually be made in this life. That is the substance for

---

[putting sin to death] there is "an habitual weakening of it." Further, (continued on the next page) he writes, "the first thing in mortification is the weakening of this habit, that it shall not impel...this is called 'crucifying the flesh with the lusts thereof'" John Owen *The Mortification of Sin*. Christian Focus: Fearn Ross-shire (1996) pp. 64–67.

which I have been contending. On the other hand, what I have been decrying is that low view of God's work in redeemed hearts that expects the Christian counselor to accomplish very little. Often this is not expressed in so many words, but that is what the counselor expects and the impression he conveys by what he says – or leaves unsaid! That erroneous view must be countered, and the full potential for personal growth in overcoming sin that the New Testament describes must be held forth.

Let every counselor keep in mind that both he and his counselees may always accomplish more than they actually do. Neither one is perfect! That they must continue to grow in their abilities to appropriate God's truth in this life is a given. Now, that is not because of the failure of the new heart. It is not because of failure to do much for the counselee that it does not come anywhere near perfection in this life. On the contrary, the seeming lack of progress is due to the fact that the regenerate person has such a long way to go *because he began at such a low point!* The pit from which he was dug was very deep. Paul says that "those who are in the flesh can't please God" (Romans 8:8). It is a long distance from unregenerate to regenerate living. It is not that so little progress is made by the new heart; rather, it is that so much progress is needed! *Everything* must change: "you must no longer walk like the Gentiles do" (Ephesians 4:17). That is the problem: the required change is a large order.

Now, add to that the fact that so many counselors have very low expectations for change, and you have a sorry mix to overcome. But the resources of God are more than adequate to enable you to raise your expectations. That is the point. Recognizing this, there is every reason to strongly encourage you to forge ahead toward expecting significant change. Only then, as you come to believe that God's Word can make outstanding differences in people with new hearts, is true change likely to occur.

"But if it is mere habit that is behind a counselee's problems..."

Whoa! Let's avoid that question-begging epithet, "mere." I once had a philosophy teacher at Johns Hopkins University who would never fail to come down hard on those who use the word "mere" to disparage a concept in which he believed. Professor George Boaz said that if we are not careful to watch out for such terms, we will have our beliefs eroded by such qualifying terms rather than by solid arguments. The word "mere" must not be used in the context at hand. It was, for instance, by *habit* that David came to commit adultery and murder. Surely the habits of sexual indulgence with many wives that had already become a part of his life led him to covet Bathsheba rather than turn away from what he saw. This, in turn, led to adultery and murder. And those acts led to a period of time in his life through which he suffered greatly from a bad conscience (cf. Psalms 51, 38).

Ultimately, he repented under the powerful counseling of Nathan the prophet! In that repentance, he not only revealed his sin and guilt to the world (and all posterity), but wrote graphically about his misery for the benefit of others. His words are a strong incentive to avoid the problems he encountered as the result of his unconfessed iniquity. Indeed, as he said, he was anxious to "teach transgressors" God's ways (Psalm 51:13). As heinous as the acts of this regenerate man were, his new heart is clearly seen writing such things in these two penitential Psalms. Certainly, there is nothing of perfectionism in what I have been saying, but there *is* much hope of counselees avoiding sin and amending matters when they fall into it. *That* is the major import of what you must learn and teach. We must never give up hope for genuine believing counselees – even when things go terribly wrong!

Always remember David!

Chapter Twelve

New Hearts/New Starts

I have said that, in counseling regenerate persons, the Christian counselor has a great advantage over other counselors. I have also mentioned the fact that, like Paul, the person with a new heart inwardly wants to do God's will – even though his best resolutions may end up foiled. I spoke also of possible resistance which, in some cases, may look as if there has been no change at all; the desire to please God by doing His will doesn't seem to be present. Moreover, I pointed out that in such instances the problem may stem from discouragement and frustration over past failures. But there are other kinds of circumstances as well that may account for resistance to God's Word.

The first of the possible causes of a lack of the kind of inward desire that Paul mentions in Romans 7 is that the counselee may have wrongly informed the counselor about his faith. He may have either purposely deceived him for some personal advantage ("I want to marry Mary, and she won't get married unless she can marry a Christian"), or he may have deceived himself (thinking that walking down the aisle of a church makes one a Christian). Whatever the cause, because a counselor cannot read another's heart, as we have seen, he may have been misled about his counselee's salvation. If he is not a believer, he does not have a new heart, his inner disposition is opposed to the things of God, and he wants to do his own will

– not God's. There is no wonder, in such cases, that the counselor will meet resistance to biblical directions. At length, because of the lack of a "mind" oriented toward pleasing God and because of the counselee's inability to do the will of God, a wise counselor will investigate the salvation of the counselee in greater depth than he did at the outset. In discovering that his faith is deficient he will alter his approach; instead of going on with counseling, he will begin to evangelize him. He knows that it is only possible to reach out to regenerate believers and make contact with an inner desire to please the Lord.

There are other reasons than a failure to understand salvation through Jesus Christ that bring about resistance. Principal among these is what has been designated by some as the problem of "dead wood." Some counselees appear to be unregenerate, but they are true Christians in spite of this. The difficulty is that at one time they vibrantly sought to please God by doing all those things that they were commanded. Lacking know-how, they fell flat on their faces. This failure led to a degree of disillusionment, but did not stop them in their tracks. However, continued failures over the years did. Eventually, they stopped trying to do as the Bible commands because somewhere along the line they concluded that they *could* not. So, they gave up and went to sleep on the pew. They were soon labeled "dead wood." But these persons are not dead. They are only sidetracked. Good counseling that appeals to the new life within, however low the fires may be burning, will often stir hope into a blaze once more. It is this appeal to what once glowed so brightly that will make the difference.

When necessary, as an aid to reaching the new heart, the Christian counselor has another factor that he may bring into counseling: he can circumvent the counselee and appeal to the Spirit within. Since the unregenerate counselees down the block do not have the Spirit, their counselors have no such option – even if they wished to avail themselves of it. But through prayer, the Christian counselor may go directly to God the Spirit Who is the One Who (ultimately) brings about the changes anyway. This advantage is vast: as he asks the Spirit to make the counselee willing, he is enlisting the power of God Almighty to stir those embers. By doing so, the counselor makes connection with the principal Person in the battle, since we know that the Holy Spirit fights against the flesh (Galatians 5:16ff.). He is not dependent upon the efforts of the counselee alone. Not only does the Spirit possess unlimited wisdom and might, so as to be able to respond properly and powerfully, the Spirit also works in the life of the counselee to revive him. He is the One Who brings about repentance and faith; He is the One Who brings about victory over the flesh. The body may be "dead" because of sin, but the Spirit revivifies it so that it may be used in the service of Christ (Romans 8:10). As a result, counselees need no longer be disheartened so as to lag in their spiritual growth; they may become "more than conquerors" (Romans 8:37).

When a counselor understands and believes these things, he will come to counseling armed with right attitudes and great expectations. Given the resources that are available to him, he may be able to help many with new hearts who have been called "dead wood" to make new starts!

Chapter Thirteen

Some Practical Suggestions

How can you best take advantage of your advantages? How can you reach out and make contact with that aspect of your counselee's new heart that wants to serve Christ? That is a very practical and important matter to consider. In this chapter I have tried to open up some possibilities along those lines. You will probably not want to use anything that I have written verbatim but will want to adopt the same or similar approaches, using your own words. Perhaps the most valuable asset of the chapter will be to stir up your own thinking about the matter.

It might be good to appeal to the new heart in the initial stages of the first counseling session. Here are a few ways in which to do so:

> Bill, I'm so glad you came for help. As your pastor, I've watched your Christian life progress over the years and have been delighted to see the growth that's taken place. Whatever problem brought you here today – no matter how serious – it can be solved by the power of the same Spirit Who has already made significant changes in you.

By alluding to past successes, the counselor not only brings up the fact that he believes the counselee is a Christian but, in addition, he reminds him of the fact that he has the Spirit of God in his life to bring about needed changes.

Here's another:

> Mary, I know it's hard to face the death of your husband in an automobile accident, but it's good to know that you have all of the resources of God upon which to draw. We're going to call upon just about all of them during these counseling sessions, and though the problem is great, His resources are greater still.

In this way, the counselor acknowledges and does not minimize the difficulty of the situation. But he also assures Mary that God's resources for helping her are available and more than adequate to help.

Consider the following:

> I agree with all that you've said. Your circumstances are hard to bear. But isn't it good that God knows all about them and cares? And you must remember, it is He Who is on your side to enable you to fight against all of the temptations that will overtake you in the months to come. He certainly is up to the task.

Again, notice that the emphasis falls upon God and His resources; not upon the counselor. Take another:

> No, your problem isn't impossible. Hard? Yes. Impossible? No. Not only is God able to help you to overcome it, He has already given you a new heart with the right attitudes and basic desire to do so. With that combination, there isn't any reason why you can't solve it in a half dozen weeks or so.

And one more:

> We are beginning these sessions with a great advantage over the counseling that unbelievers receive. Your new

heart that God gave you when you were born again, the Spirit dwelling within you, and the Scriptures to guide you all provide a formidable combination. There is every reason, therefore, to expect that the problems you have delineated can be solved completely.

In the midst of the counseling sessions a reminder is often needed:

> Barb, there isn't the slightest reason for your current discouragement. God has already done so much for you that you should expect even more. He has given you the correct understanding of what He requires, and when we began you stated your desire to achieve it. Now that a slight setback has occurred, there is no excuse for giving up. Because God gave you a new heart to please Him, you must focus upon doing so. Remember your intention to please Him and repent of the current sin. So let's get back to work. There is every reason to expect significant results.

And this:

> Mark, you have already come a long way. Your progress demonstrates that what God has done to change you makes it possible for you to make spiritual progress. Your understanding of the Bible is outstanding; and the probability for doing all that you have learned is great. All you have to do now is avail yourself of the many additional resources that God has placed at your disposal.

Or,

> Good. You have overcome some of the minor problems that you presented. Now it's time to tackle the big one. Are you ready? Let's check out what it will take and what you have to overcome it. To do so will require

a correct heart orientation (meaning the right goals, attitudes, and intents), a power to motivate and enable you to do all that you must, and a set of directions that will guide you in the proper course. From your outlook (or orientation) it seems that God has surely done a work in your heart. The Spirit dwells within to strengthen and empower you. And you have the Bible for a guide to direct you in God's ways. Nothing more is necessary. Let's get to work!

Then, there's the last session, terminating counseling:

You've done well, Art. You've availed yourself of most of the resources that God has provided and made good progress. Don't forget to continue to do this in the future. You will need to remember how you used Scripture in the power of the Spirit to overcome your problems. There isn't anything that lies ahead of you that you won't want to handle the same way. And, so long as you keep the same attitude of willingness to submit to God's Word, you will continue to please Him. God bless.

These scenarios are but a few examples of ways in which the resources of the Christian may be brought forward to reassure counselees that there is good reason for them to expect to make progress. Because expectations are so important to counseling, you should use them to the full whenever necessary to encourage and otherwise motivate counselees.

Chapter Fourteen

Heart-to-Heart Talk

I have already mentioned the fact that the Bible pictures the fool trying to talk himself into believing that "there is no God" (Psalm 14:1). In this passage, something that is widely recognized is made clear: we all talk to ourselves, as the Bible puts it, in our hearts. Most people have learned to do so quietly, but there are some who never did; instead, they mumble or otherwise talk to themselves out loud. And some, without making a sound, talk by moving their lips silently framing, but not speaking, the words. However you do it, into whichever category of self-talkers you may fall, *you do it* – all the time.

Not a day goes by in which you do not carry on many conversations with yourself about all sorts of matters. And you do so in your heart. "Now let's see," you ask yourself, "what is it that I have to buy at the grocery store?" The first thing you know, you are making a list in your head. If it becomes too long, you may commit the list to writing so you will not forget any of the items that you want. But the list making begins in your head (we say "head" where the biblical writers would have said "heart!")[37] You lie awake on your bed at night, unable to get to sleep. So you begin to talk to yourself. Perhaps you review the day that has just passed; possibly you begin to think, plan, or even worry about tomorrow. One way

---

37 Remember, in Scripture the two are equated.

to think is to talk over matters internally. Indeed, thinking always involves such heart talk. Obviously, then, heart talk is important. Here, if any place, is where you have your deepest "heart-to-heart talks" with yourself! Your heart talks to itself. The question is: what does it say?

It is vital, therefore, for you to guard your self-talk. Most people take care about what they say openly, audibly. They have learned to do so because verbalizing out loud what one thinks can bring dire consequences. Others may challenge you, get angry with you, or contradict you. So, early on, most people learn not to equate heart talk with mouth talk. That means that they think they can get away with saying what they say in their hearts. ("I'd like to strangle her if I had half a chance!") Consequently, they rarely put the same sort of guard upon their hearts that they put upon their lips. In heart talk one is likely to let down his hair, to lower the bars. Therein lies the danger in inner dialog.

Actually, as we can see in Psalm 14:1, people don't really "get away with" heart talk after all. God monitors the heart and knows all that one says to himself. And, of course, when you stop to think about it, what God hears you saying is much more important than what others hear! So good counselors warn counselees about the dangers inherent in heart talk. Because having heart-to-heart talks with one's self is inevitable, they encourage counselees to speak truth to themselves. Psalm 15:2 applauds the one "who walks with integrity, and works righteousness, and speaks truth in his heart." The three things go together. The walking and the working are the outcome of the speaking.

The warnings that you give to counselees, counselor, need not be your own; sometimes the best thing is to simply refer to what God says:

Beware that there is no base thought in your heart.
                    Deuteronomy 15:9

> Do not let them say in their heart "Aha, our desire!"
> Psalm 35:25

> Transgression speaks to the ungodly within his heart.
> Psalm 36:1

Transgression is but an abstraction which is here personified. In this context it means that thoughts of transgressing God's will are first spoken and pondered in one's heart. But the one who speaks is the one whose heart (here personified as if transgression were an actual person) speaks to itself. In the heart, then, is the place to defeat transgression before it flows out into words and actions. (For more, compare such passages as Isaiah 14:13; 47:8, 10; Romans 10:6; Revelation 18:7.)

What people ought to be saying in their hearts is "Let us now fear the Lord our God" (cf. Jeremiah 5:24). So, since it is clear that God acknowledges the existence of and monitors and is concerned about heart talk, we too must become concerned.

It might be enlightening as well as fruitful for your counselee who is having trouble in this area to keep a record of his heart talk. He will often forget, engage in it unconsciously, and so on. But to the extent that he is able to monitor it, he is likely to become more careful about what he says to himself. Indeed, if he also records some pertinent passage of Scripture along with the entry, that may make him begin to bring the Bible into the discussion whenever he talks to himself. As a result he will learn to keep transgression at arm's length or counter its words with God's Word. And if he brings you a full and honest written report, you may learn some things about what is going on inside his mind. At any rate, it is important at times to discuss self-talk with your counselee.

In one area, in speaking to someone who was a part of a vice squad, I confirmed what I had found true in counseling: persons who commit acts of pedophilia do so only after much inner consultation. They must convince themselves that, in their cases, it would be all right. They need to reach a point where they have justified the act to themselves: "That little girl is flaunting her sexuality; she's asking for it!" or "My wife won't give me sex; I'm entitled to get it somewhere," etc. Before the first act, usually a good bit of time is spent in such self-talk. It is important, then, to teach counselees to nip their problems in the bud. That means, in the heart.

Of course, this sin is not the only one that counselees contemplate in their hearts before entering into the act. But it is often the sort of sin that one would not discuss with others.

Chapter Fifteen
What's In It for Your Counselees?

That is to say, if the heart is so important (and we have seen it is), and if from it flow all matters in one's life[38] (and we have seen that they do), then the next question is: "What is in your counselee's heart?" What may be found there is that upon which he meditates, that which lends guidance in his decision-making, and that which dominates his thinking. It will have a lot to do with how he receives your counsel and what he does with it.

If a counselee's heart is filled with the Scriptures as the basis for all considerations that are made by it, then counseling will eventuate in good results; if his heart is filled with wickedness or self then it will eventuate in very different results. So, as a Christian counselor, you must take pains to fill your counselee's heart with God's Word. Doing so will replace wrong thoughts as truth drives them from his heart.

John Calvin wrote:

For a number may imagine of their own brain what the law of God is, but in the meanwhile it standeth so with them, that when we behold their life and conversation [lifestyle], it appeareth that they have profited no whit at all in his school. It is meet therefore that our heart be brought to the school of God, to wit, that whatsoever

---

38 Proverbs 4:23.

he teacheth us, it may be thoroughly imprinted and engraven within. [39]

The Psalmist puts it this way: "The law of his God [Scripture] is in his heart; his steps do not slip" (Psalm 37:31). Clearly, the writer sees a vital connection between the Word of God in the heart and the lifestyle of the one in whom it is found. The word torah ("law") has in it the picture of one thrusting forth his finger so as to point the way. The concept of guidance is inherent in it. So to avoid slipping into sin and its consequences, he will need to thoroughly ingest biblical principles.

Having the law in the heart is not merely a matter of knowledge, it leads to healthy attitudes as well: "I delight to do Your will, O my God; Your law is within my heart" (Psalm 40:8). It is not mere memorization of the Bible that the Psalmist is talking about. No. He has something more in mind. He has so assimilated the teaching of the Bible that it has become woven into the fabric of his thought-processes. It has become the essence of his worldview, his outlook on all of life. His heart is so impregnated by biblical thinking that whenever there is an opportunity to use biblical thought for purposes of decision-making and action on his part, it is a joy for him to do so. He loves to see the Scriptures at work. There is a "delight" that nothing else equals. He declares, "I have inherited Your testimonies forever, for they are the joy of my heart." He rejoices in understanding God's truth and delights in pleasing God by acting in accordance with God's Word. How is that?

The joy that having one's heart full of God's Word is in knowing that one is thinking and walking in God's straight way: "The precepts of the Lord are right, rejoicing the heart; the commandment of the Lord is pure, enlightening the eyes" (Psalm 19:8). He has knowledge not only about salvation, but also about the world in which he lives. The person void of God's revelation does not possess anything like

---

39 John Calvin, *Sermons on Psalm 119*. Old Paths Pubs.: Audubon (1966), p. 19.

it. He doesn't know the most fundamental matters of all: where the universe came from, why it (he) is here, and where it is all heading. His ignorance is almost tangible!

Because of the importance of what is in the heart of a counselee, counselors tell their counselees, "Apply your heart to discipline and your ears to words of knowledge" (Proverbs 23:12), and point them to the Scriptures that are appropriate to their problems. Counselors know that as "Oil and perfume make the heart glad, so a man's counsel is sweet to his friend" (Proverbs 27:9). Therefore, the biblical counselor understands how important his task is and how vital it is for him to give biblical counsel to his counselees.

The upshot of these facts is simply this: the counselor must know his own Bible well enough to be able to retrieve and utilize the proper and appropriate verses for each counselee that fit his situation. And he must be able to convince his counselee to treasure God's Word in his heart that he may not sin against Him (Psalm 119:11). In other words, counseling is biblical when it permeates the thought and the actions of both the counselor and the counselee.

But – and here I must strongly urge you to be cautious – that does not mean piling verse after verse upon counselees as if the quantity of Scripture used is what makes the difference. The tendency for novice counselors to do this seems to be almost universal. But it is a dangerous and mistaken one. Why do counselors do so? Probably for good and bad reasons. Because some know that it is God's Word that transforms people they think that the more Scripture they quote the more likely they are to help. Others simply don't know how to interpret Scripture and apply it. So, they hope against hope that some verse they quote will catch fire and make the difference.

But, while God can use His Word any way He wishes – and often He is better to us than we deserve – that is not the way to minister the Bible. Rather the Scriptures must be "opened" (Luke

24:32). This "opening" consists of so showing what a passage means that the listener not only understands the passage, but sees that it is exactly what God was saying and not merely the ideas of the counselor. In this way, its full force of divine authority shines forth from the passage.

Having opened the Scriptures, the counselor also needs to be able to apply them to the counselee's situation. That is to say, he must be able to show the relevance of the passage to the circumstances in which the counselee finds himself. In doing so, he must be very careful not to twist passages of Scripture to "fit." Unfortunately, many do so. This happens when they do not know the Bible well enough themselves. For counselors to be able to apply God's Word properly, then, they must be familiar with a wide range of biblical teaching. This will not come over night, but as the faithful counselor spends time studying the Scriptures on his own (using references and commentaries; not merely reading), and as he studies the Bible in relationship to every case he is carrying at any given time, he will find his knowledge increasing. What is needed is not counselors who know only what the latest book about counseling has to say (not even mine) but who increasingly know what God's Word teaches. The counselor, as well as the counselee, therefore, must have God's Word firmly fixed in his heart.

How does a counselor encourage his counselees to hide God's Word in their hearts? He may spend time talking about the importance of doing so. That has its place. But the most forceful way in which to show the importance of the Scriptures is to help deliver him from some difficulty by their application in such a way that he sees that God's Word is not only true but practical. When following Scripture makes a difference, that fact impresses itself upon a counselee more strongly than all the exhortations of the counselor ever could. So, when one is helped by following the Bible, make a point that it was the truth of God that brought about the helpful change. Don't take personal credit for what God did through His Word. Whatever you do, exalt God's Word as God Himself does in the Bible! There is great joy in counseling this way because you have the opportunity to exalt God for what He has done for your counselee.

Chapter Sixteen

Knowledge of Sin

In the last chapter I spoke about getting Scripture into the heart of counselees in order to bring about the needed changes that will cause the believer's spiritual growth. Now that doesn't happen automatically. To begin with, the process of change requires a standard held up against the life of the counselee. When he has such a standard – rather than searching for some supposed "idol" – he may easily understand what in his life honors God and what does not.

Paul put it this way: "I wouldn't have known what was sin except by law [Scripture]" (Romans 7:7). That still is the factor that makes the difference. It is only as one understands and applies the Scriptures to his own life that he is able to determine what is sin and what is righteousness. The Scriptures set forth God's holy will for man. If we fail to do as He says, that's sin. If we do what He forbids, that also is sin. It is not difficult to discover what needs correction if one seeks the answers in God's written revelation, the standard He has graciously given to us.

But sadly, too many people seem to think that they can determine what God's will is on their own initiative, without consulting the Scriptures. Those who do not like a standard imposed upon them rebel against having to submit to biblical teaching. On the other hand, there are legalists who love rules so much that they want to define, delineate, and demand far-ranging (and often highly dubious) implications of the biblical standard. People at both extremes have problems accepting the standard that God provided "as is."

The person who wants to become his own rule maker (and there are not a few among those who call themselves Christians) will argue with counselors when they bring the Scriptures to bear upon their cases. They will make excuses, interpose other ideas foreign to Scripture, and do whatever it takes to maintain their vaunted autonomy. This desire for autonomy is itself sin, and they must be faced with that fact. It was what plunged the human race into sin in the first place when Adam and Eve determined to decide for themselves what was the right way rather than accepting and abiding by God's clearly expressed standard. Holding up this fact against their insistence upon having their own way is necessary to combat autonomy today. When the counselee explains, "But I think…" he should be faced with such verses as Proverbs 3:5, 6, 14:12, and Isaiah 53:6. Part of the counseling task is to help him change his attitude from "I think" to "God says."[40] Because it is a large part of the counseling task to help move counselee's from the former attitude to the latter you must work at ways of doing so.

On the other hand, there are those who, either on their own or as the result of the teaching of some church or group, add to the scriptural standard. They find themselves tightly wrapped up in matters that Paul would have dismissed as indifferent. These actions become matters of sin only if they do them in opposition to what they believe God's will to be. Someone holding contrary views may lead them to violate their consciences by encouraging

---

[40] I am greatly troubled when I hear a preacher say from the pulpit "I believe" or "I think." He is not the standard-giver for his congregation. He should always hold up God's Word – and nothing else – as their standard. I would much rather hear him say such things as "God says in this passage," or "Here is what God requires; let me read it for you," or words to that effect.

them to engage in what they believe or think to be wrong. That means that their hearts are led into sinning by another who has no such scruples. In either case, the sin would not have been in the act itself, but in the attitude of the one who, while thinking it was sin (or might be sin) indulged in it anyway. Paul discussed this issue in Romans 14 where he concluded that "whatever is not of faith is sin."

So, the first task of the counselor is to bring Scripture into vital contact with the new heart that is oriented toward pleasing God. In doing so, whenever it is necessary, he will spend time explaining what is and is not sin, according to the Scriptures. Because of the habits of autonomy brought over into the new life, and the legalism of those who add to the Bible, this may occupy more time than you might suppose. Clearly, Scripture alone, properly interpreted and applied, must be the only standard by which to determine the will of God. If any other standard is brought into the picture – or allowed – it will do more harm than good. Thus, the counselor himself must be a good interpreter of the Bible and insist upon accurate interpretation by counselees as well. For the counselor to know the Bible well enough to bring the proper passages to every counseling case, no matter what the difficulty may be, is one of the great joys of biblical counseling. The counselor knows that he is applying the correct remedy to his counselee because it is God's Word, not his own. And he can expect God's Spirit to use His Word.

Chapter Seventeen

Obey From the Heart

We have seen already that in your Christian counselees there is a new disposition of the heart to which you may appeal. That, of itself, should give you a cheerful outlook on counseling. Your counselee has a basic orientation toward doing God's will, and by regeneration, God has changed him so as to be able to do it. Moreover, he has the Spirit of God within to enlighten and empower him. If you were dealing with unbelievers, you would have none of the above assets to assist you in counseling. Indeed, it would be fruitless to attempt to get counselees to do God's will when they cannot (remember Romans 8:8). Of course, they may for a time, and in a way, *outwardly* conform to the biblical standard, but it is impossible for them to make the heart-change that God requires. The outlook for all such attempts is gloomy.

Yet, it is necessary to urge true believers as well to be sure that their conformity to God's will is not hypocritical. They don't automatically do God's will from the heart. The Pharisee looked good on the outside of the cup but was filthy within. He was a whitewashed grave with only death and corruption inside. Of course, you are not working with unregenerate Pharisees. However, because a believer was born with a nature that is corrupt and oriented toward deceitfulness (remember Jeremiah 17:9), he may have developed patterns of responding toward others, toward God, and even toward himself that are deceptive (cf. James 1:26). It is, therefore, essential to urge counselees to "obey from the heart" (Romans 6:17).[41] What does that expression mean? It speaks of genuineness, reality. It is obedience that is contrary to all deception.

The Scriptures set forth this idea of genuineness in other ways as well. Peter, for instance, speaks of "stirring up" Christians' "sincere minds." The writer of Hebrews speaks of "a true heart" that is "sprinkled to rid us of an evil conscience" (Hebrews 10:22). Peter also writes of "having cleansed yourselves by obedience to the truth" so that "you can have brotherly affection without pretense" (I Peter 1:22). In all of these passages, it is assumed that it is possible for Christians to think and act genuinely. They do not have to continue patterns of deception and outward conformity to God's Word. Jesus Christ freed them from slavery to sin (Romans 6:6). Assume and expect genuineness from counselees because it is what the Bible teaches that you ought to expect; and build this expectation into counselees as well. Some counselees are discouraged by past failures (as we have seen) and have given up hope of truth in the inner person. There is no excuse for this (cf. Galatians 6:9).

You cannot enforce sincerity, but you can urge it (Acts 11:23). And you can warn against deception. But you must take the word of the counselee for what he says since you cannot look into his heart. As we have seen, that territory belongs to God alone. We can be sure that He will deal with what he finds there in a satisfactory manner (cf. Psalm 66:18; Matthew 18:35).

So, while there is every expectation of a genuine response to God's Word when you present it to Christian counselees, it is by no means assured that this is what you will receive. When, in time, the evidence turns up that the counselee has falsified his words (which

---

41 Here, the context indicates this obedience is obedience to the gospel message: i.e., obeying by faith. But the expression still carries the idea of genuineness. There are, sadly, many false professions of faith. In part, this is due to flawed presentations of the gospel.

may be revealed by his later confession or by unfulfilled homework, etc.), you must call for repentance (cf. Psalm 51:17). Upon genuine repentance (which is evidenced by fruit that is appropriate to it; see Matthew 3:8; Luke 3:8), encourage the counselee to become the genuine person that God wants him to be. In this way, his works will not be "dead works" designed to impress others but righteous deeds wrought by the Spirit within in order to please God.

In some ways what goes on in the heart is even more important than the outer action. When God refused to allow David to build His temple, he noted that the desire in his heart to do so was right and good (I Kings 8:17, 18). God acknowledges those worthy intentions that we may have, but that He does not allow us to accomplish. Now, of course, that is no excuse for failure to do what He requires when He gives us both the intention and the opportunity to do it for Him. But, if both are not possible, you can see that the inner desire of the heart is noted and commended by God. This fact may be of importance in counseling those who, for various unforeseen circumstances, are not able to do all that they desire to do for God (becoming missionaries, writing a book, etc.). At any rate, it is comforting for counselors to be able to tell counselees that, because God is the Heart-Knower, He is able to commend them for their best intentions that He does not allow them to fulfill.

Chapter Eighteen

Experiencing the Joy of Counseling

Not only in its title, but throughout this book, I have referred to the joy that Christian counselors may experience by doing biblical counseling. It is time to sum up a few of those comments and to introduce a few more.

You will remember how we saw that there is joy in seeing God work through His Word. Counseling often gets more visible and more immediate results than preaching does, as counselors help people move from sorrow, fear, anguish, or other states of misery to places of victory, peace, and satisfaction. Being there when this happens, as participants in the ministry of that Word, seeing God bring about these significant changes is no small matter. Few activities provide more direct experience of what we preach about all the time.[42] Preachers who do not counsel miss one of the main joys of the ministry. Others who might counsel informally, but do not, also miss out on this joy. If you have never experienced the blessings of such a privilege, it is time for you to do so, thereby

---

42 Ours is an age that bases much on experience. Scripture is often bypassed in search of experiences. That is certainly not our interest or concern in stressing the experience the counselor receives from "rejoicing with those who rejoice." While experience may never be the basis for doctrine or life, it is not wrong to enjoy the experiences that come as a result of following that Word.

Joyfully Counseling People with New Hearts

entering into the happiness of watching God transform lives right there in front of your eyes! Determine to start counseling today!

If you have never known the joy to which I am referring, let me introduce you to Paul, the joyous counselor. That may not be the way in which you would think of him because the facts about his extensive counseling activity have been rarely pointed out. For starters, listen to him, as he writes:

> …you are in our hearts to die together and to live together. I have a lot of confidence in you; I have a lot of pride in you. I am full of encouragement; in spite of all of our afflictions, I am thoroughly delighted…I am now delighted – not that you were pained, but that your pain led to repentance.
>
> II Corinthians 7:3, 4, 9

Here we encounter the apostle elated that his counsel, given in I Corinthians, led to wonderful changes in the lives of members of the church at Corinth. It is important to notice that in II Corinthians he chronicles not only the change, but how it affected him. Titus had returned with the good news about the repentance that had taken place (7:13), and the Apostle, who had been quite apprehensive about the response to his counsel in his first epistle, tells us that he was "delighted" by what Titus told him. This is the sort of joy that the biblical counselor receives when his counselees respond in ways that show Scripture has penetrated their hearts and motivated them to obey God.

So far as Titus, himself, was concerned, the joy spilled over upon him as well: "his emotions" became "all the warmer," Paul says, as he spoke about "the obedience that you all showed as you received him with fear and trembling" (v. 15). Paul concludes that discussion by saying, "I am delighted that in every way I can put my confidence in you!" (v. 16).

What do you think of that? Isn't there something grand to the fact that great joy results from biblical counseling? Was this a one time experience? Listen to Paul again, this time writing to the church at Thessalonica:

> What is our hope or joy or winner's wreath about which we shall boast? Isn't it you?...Yes, you are our glory and joy.
> I Thessalonians 2:19, 20

Paul once again is exulting in God's blessing on his ministry. And listen to this:

> How can we ever thank God adequately for you for all of the joy that we have experienced because of you in the presence of our God?
> I Thessalonians 3:9

You can see from these brief excerpts that what I have been talking about was a reality in the ministry of the apostle, can't you? Why not in yours as well?

Was Paul unique in this regard? Not at all. Here is how the Apostle John writes to a convert of his who has done the right thing in the face of great trial:

> I say this because I was delighted when the brothers came and testified about your truth, that you are walking in the truth. Nothing pleases me more than to hear that my own children[43] are walking in the truth.
> III John 3, 4

In a serious misuse of church discipline by Diotrephes, Gaius, to whom John wrote, had been expelled from his church. On pain of excommunication, Diotrephes, doubtless the pastor of Gaius' church, had refused to allow anyone to receive traveling missionaries into his home.[44] But Gaius received them

---
43 That is, his "child" in the faith. Cf. Philemon 10.
44 According to John, this misuse consisted of using discipline for one's own advantage.

anyway. John commends him: "Dear friend, you are faithful when you do anything for the brothers" (v. 5) and rejoices over his actions.

Obviously, in spite of suffering, heartache, and eventual death, the apostles found the results of their work in the lives of their sheep a comforting and encouraging aspect of what they did.

Now, the joy of counseling comes not only from seeing God work in the lives of counselees, but also from knowing that you are doing something important for God. This joy comes not from recognizing your importance, however, but from a recognition of the fact that God is working through a clay vessel like you to help others. Biblical counseling is His work; you are one of those He has sovereignly determined to use to bless others through your ministry. That ought to be heartening. How is that? So many counselors out there in the world, following Freud, Rogers, or some other unbelieving theorist are never sure that their analysis of the human condition is correct. They see that they may be able to help people temporarily over some hump or other. However, if and when they reflect about what they do, they surely can recognize something of the futility of it. Those who do stop to ponder can easily come to many of the same conclusions that Solomon did. He tells us that all that is done under the sun is "vanity." The Hebrew word translated vanity has the meaning of something that is useless to do because its results are not permanent.[45]

In contrast, you know that every advance that your counselees make in their lives has eternal consequences (not to speak of the heavenly benefits *you* will reap). This makes your work more than a job that is done for nothing other than temporal reasons. What you do, if you think about it, will not only bless counselees, their families and their churches here and now (itself no mean accomplishment); it will honor God Who, in turn, will reward them in ways that are

---

45 For details, see my commentary on Ecclesiastes, Life under the Sun/Son.

consistent with the changes that they make. Isn't that something in which to "delight" (as Paul put it)?

And, lastly, don't forget that in biblical counseling, you are a fellow-worker with the Holy Spirit. What a privilege! Think about it for a moment. Paul was pleased to be able to do so. Here is what he wrote: "We are God's co-workers; you are God's field, God's building" (I Corinthians 3:9). In working to build up the saints (or to cultivate fruit in their lives) you have the great joy and honor of becoming a "co-worker" (fellow-worker) with God! Paul alluded to this fact in persuading his counselees to follow God's will: "We also urge you as God's co-workers not to receive God's grace in vain" (II Corinthians 6:1). Then at last, when he saw God at work in their lives, he could say, "we are glad when we are weak and you are strong, and what we pray for is that you may be fully restored" (II Corinthians 13:9). Once more Paul refers to their response to the counsel he gave them as bringing "gladness" to himself.

What made the apostles so sensitive to the welfare of their counselees that they would rejoice or sorrow according to how they responded to their counsel? Paul said when writing to the church at Philippi, "I thank my God every time I remember you, always in every request…making the request with joy.…It is right for me to think this about all of you, because I have you in my heart" (Philippians 1:3, 4, 7). There you have it – Paul had his counselees in his heart! When you counsel that way, you will begin to know something of the joys of counseling.

Chapter Nineteen
Conclusion

I have considered enough of the important matters concerning the new heart in the believer to provide a clear idea of how biblical counseling ought to proceed. In addition, I have tried to show that these facts should lead to anticipation not only of satisfaction on the part of the Christian counselor, but even more – it should lead to joyful counseling! I have attempted to set forth Scriptural information that leads to this view and have urged all pastors, elders, and others to join in the work. I have tried to show that one of the significant failures of our counseling, even in biblical circles, stems from low, unbiblical expectations, and I have attempted to correct misconceptions in an effort to declare the truth of the matter.

Whether I have succeeded in my efforts remains to be seen. The proof that I have done so will be in the number of believers who, for the first time, take up the work of counseling. Let me assure you one last time – you are missing one of the greatest blessings a Christian may experience: seeing God change lives under your ministry of His Word. As John the Apostle, near the end of his long life of living for Christ, said, "Nothing pleases me more than to hear that my own children are walking in the truth" (III John 4). Are you missing the pleasure about which he wrote? Consider the matter and make the right decision.

Conclusion

    Those of you who are already engaged in counseling, learn to enjoy the work as you undertake it with the highest expectations. God will bless your efforts, and you will be blessed as you do so.

www.ingramcontent.com/pod-product-compliance
Lightning Source LLC
Chambersburg PA
CBHW071309110426
42743CB00042B/1231